A WORLD OUT OF TIME

MADAGASCAR

AERIAL VIEW OF TSINGY DE BEMARAHA, A PLATEAU OF ERODING LIMESTONE PINNACLES.

ILLE SAINCT Lorens
Madagascar

MADAGASCAR ACCORDING TO A MAP BY E. LE TESTU, 1555, COPYRIGHT 1884.

A WORLD OUT OF TIME

MADAGASCAR

Photographs and Text by
FRANS LANTING

Introduction by Gerald Durrell
Essays by Alison Jolly and John Mack

Aperture

Backed by otherworldly vegetation from the spiny desert, an Antandroy tribesman holds an egg laid by the largest bird that ever lived. Aepyornis maximus, *also known as the elephant bird, was a flightless giant 2.5 meters tall and weighing 300 kilograms. It became extinct several hundred years ago, but some Malagasy still remember* Aepyornis *in name as "vorombe," big bird. Whole eggs are still found on occasion after heavy rains expose them in sandy stream beds.*

SCATTERING CLOUDS OF A STORM FRONT DRIFT ACROSS THE INDIAN OCEAN

CONTENTS

This publication is underwritten in part by the Professional Photography Division of Eastman Kodak Company through its continuing support of photography in journalism.

INTRODUCTION

Gerald Durrell

I once described Madagascar as being shaped like a badly made omelette lying off the east coast of Africa but containing—as a properly made omelette should—a wealth of good things inside it.

My wife and I have been lucky enough to have visited and studied this, the world's fourth largest island, over a number of years, and each time we go there we become more enchanted with its people and its fantastic flora and fauna, nearly all unique to this giant land.

Our first impressions were formed in the colorful, pulsating capital city of Antananarivo, fondly known as Tana. On market day, crowds of smiling Malagasy make their way down the central boulevard and side streets as if in a bed of mushrooms: White umbrellas guard each little stall, where you can buy anything from a chile to a chicken. The Malagasy are an elegant mix of cultures and races, and whether you are in Tana or a remote coastal village, the cheerfulness and courtesy with which you are greeted are remarkable.

Madagascar's best-known animals are the ring-tailed lemurs, which saunter through the forests with great élan, a pinkish bloom to their gray fur, holding their tails aloft, bannerlike, and looking as though they have just left Aubrey Beardsley's studio after a sitting. Among the thirty or so other kinds of lemur is the indri. The size of a three-year-old child, it is impressively attired in glistening black and white fur. Its wild and haunting cries, not unlike the songs of whales, pervade the forest with a strange melancholy. But there are many other animals and plants found nowhere else in the world, such as multi-colored chameleons with swiveling eyes; and the majestic baobab trees, their swollen trunks crowned with emerald leaves.

In this book has been gathered the expertise of Dr. John Mack, who has a deep knowledge of the Malagasy people and their culture, and Dr. Alison Jolly, surely the doyenne of Madagascar's natural history, with her vast experience of its flora and fauna. Coupled with this are brilliant illustrations and text by Frans Lanting, whose photographs are so beautiful to look at that you practically hear, smell, and feel the great island as well.

This is a truly timely book, because Madagascar, its plants, its animals, and its very people are in the gravest danger. Centuries of pressures on the land from intensive farming and herding have taken their toll. Once nearly covered in trees, the island has less than a fifth of its forests left, and the denuded central region bakes like a brick in the sun.

It is essential that the rest of the world realize the biological importance of the island and the plight of its people, and hurry to the rescue of this extraordinary corner of the planet. I know this book will help achieve that result. Madagascar must be saved for the sake of the Malagasy people, for the sake of its forests and their unique inhabitants, and so that future generations may have the privilege of hearing the mournful song of the indri echoing through the green oceans of leaves.

Two drowsy sifakas (Propithecus verreauxi) *have wedged themselves in the crotch of a tamarind tree along the Mandrare River for a siesta on a hot summer's day.*

PREFACE

Frans Lanting

To Westerners, Madagascar has long been synonymous with exotica, a place at the end of the earth, the ultimate fantasy island. Like many before me, I had been lured there by this mystique when I first arrived in 1985. I found a country that had just ended a self-enforced period of political isolation from the West. Foreign travelers were rare, and only a handful of researchers and conservationists were active. From them I learned about the easiest places to fulfill my naturalist's curiosity about Madagascar's unique fauna. I've never liked the beaten path however, even when it's only lightly trodden, and in Madagascar it was tempting to stray. Following up on rumors and old accounts, I blazed my own trail. It led me to Bemaraha—an extraordinary landscape of limestone pinnacles, which if situated in North America or Europe might be as well known a landmark as Yosemite or Stonehenge. But Bemaraha's sole appointed guardian told me the last official visitor he had seen had passed through 15 years before. When I showed my photos of Bemaraha to senior government officials in Antananarivo, they expressed disbelief that such a wonder existed in their own country. I realized then that a photographer in Madagascar had more of a mission than in the West, where everything of any significance is overexposed by a multitude of media.

Few places on earth can lay better claim to the epithet of a lost world than Madagascar. Much of what has been written in the past about its natural and cultural heritage is either buried in obscure archives or out of print, inaccessible to the general public. When I began my work in 1985, only two illustrated books about the island's natural history had been published in this century. My task therefore took on the character of a rediscovery. Working in tandem with scientists, and sometimes preceding them, I came eye to eye with animals that had never been properly documented. Creatures like fossa and aye aye that live in the shadows of their own myths gave me an inkling of the exhilaration the great 19th-century naturalists must have felt when they did their pioneering work in the tropics.

Popular media like to perpetuate the myth of Western explorers venturing into virgin jungles alone. Nothing could be further from the truth in Madagascar, where, as Alison Jolly has pointed out, "the forest is networked with tracks and always we are led by a guide for whom one track is the pathway home."

Following those paths into villages adjacent to the forests so treasured by naturalists, I became involved in the lives of Malagasy people, whose impact on the island environment has been called "a tragedy without villains." Their pressing problems with everyday survival broadened my initial fascination with natural history into a perspective that incorporated their concerns. But Madagascar's economic hardship, however important as an immediate issue, doesn't fully explain the relationship between man and nature, which is rooted in a unique culture whose development mirrors the evolution of life on the Great Island. From a few cultural strands a complex fabric arose. Like lemurs, the Malagasy evolved in isolation, adapting to local circumstances in different parts of the island.

This book is dedicated to the
people of Madagascar
To those who honor the
past
To those struggling through
today
And to those working for
tomorrow.

*Ity boky ity dia atolotro ho
an'ny vahoaka Malagasy,
ho an' ireo izay manaja ny
fomban-drazana sy ny lasa,
sy ho an' ireo izay mitolona
amin'ny fiainana hatramin'izay,
ary koa ho an' ireo izay miasa
mba hitsinjovana ny ho avy.*

In the last few years Madagascar has leapt from obscurity to the limelight of
international attention. In ambitious plans aimed at stemming the tide of
environmental destruction, it is finally realized that if people are part of the
problem, they will also have to be part of the solution. To what extent
environmental action plans can dovetail rather than clash with a culture
strongly attached to ancestral traditions is a matter that has relevance far
beyond the island's shores. Madagascar can be a test case for a new approach
to development and conservation, one that addresses the needs of local people
as well as the concerns of international conservationists.

This then is the background for my book. I did not want to show lemurs by
themselves, nor man apart. Rather, I wanted to attempt a synthesis. I invited
Alison Jolly and John Mack to express their views. I did the rest. I hope the
result shows that Madagascar today transcends the interests of naturalists and
anthropologists. It is a world out of time, a micro-cosmos that shows the
wondrous creativity of the forces of nature and the human mind as nature and
culture evolve in isolation. It is also a world running out of time and shows
how dangerously close humans are to destroying the very earth that sustains
them. I hope, however, that in the years to come the people of Madagascar
will show the world that this imbalance can be redressed. The seeds of change
are there in their own wisdom, as expressed in one of their many eloquent
sayings:

The Earth is the first wife of God:
it cares for the living
and embraces the dead.

Ny tany vadíben'i Zanahary:
mihary ny velone
manotrona ny maty.

13

A grove of baobabs (Adansonia grandidieri), *leafless in winter, reveal the distinctive rootlike branches that have earned them the nickname of "upside-down tree." Seven kinds of baobabs are native to Madagascar, while all of Africa boasts only a single species.*

Confined to Madagascar, some two dozen species of lemurs survive as a separate branch of the primate family. They include the spunky black lemur (Lemur macaco), left, whose males are jet black but females rusty brown, and the elegant sifaka (Propithecus verreauxi), a mild-mannered leaf eater, right, which inhabits arid forest in the south. Once widespread in Africa and North America, lemurs were driven into oblivion by later-evolving, smarter monkeys.

Madagascar is losing its topsoil at an alarming rate. Rains leach precious minerals from deforested slopes into rivers such as the Mahajilo, which in turn stain the Indian Ocean surrounding the island a vivid red. U.S. astronauts circling the earth have remarked that Madagascar—nicknamed the Great Red Island—seems to be bleeding to death.

Madagascar's natural wealth
includes more than half the world's
chameleons. The largest may reach
70 centimeters in length and include
small birds among its prey. Here, a
Parson's chameleon (Chameleo
parsonii) scans its surroundings
with independently swiveling eyes.

OVERLEAF

Fire-resistant palms (Mademia
nobilis) are the only trees to have
survived generations of annual bush
fires on the Horombe plateau near
Isalo National Park.

Wrapped in the thin cotton garments called lambas, worn by most Malagasy, a group of highland people has gathered for an all-night wake at the house of a deceased man in Andranomadio.

OVERLEAF

Sails become tents when a group of fishermen traveling along the west coast draw their outrigger canoes up on the beach and make camp for the night along the Mozambique Channel.

THE NATURALISTS' PROMISED LAND

Alison Jolly

May I announce to you that Madagascar is the naturalists' promised land? Nature seems to have retreated there into a private sanctuary, where she could work on different models from any she has used elsewhere. There you meet bizarre and marvelous forms at every step.

PHILIPPE DE COMMERSON, 1771

After dozing in a tree cavity for most of the day, a squirrel-size sportive lemur (Lepilemur mustelinus) *emerges in late afternoon. Despite its common name, this nocturnal creature is inactive most of the time even at night, a consequence of its low-energy leaf diet.*

I f you fly into Madagascar, you pass over the Betsiboka River hemorrhaging red earth into the cobalt sea. Your plane lowers slowly over bare savannas, slashed by the red erosion gullies called lavaka. In the last moments before landing at Antananarivo, the capital, you look down on a landscape arranged in human scale. Neat squared rice paddies are cupped in the valleys. In their seasons the paddies reflect the sky in calm water-mirrors, or are jeweled with the luminous yellow-green of nursery fields, or stretch as an emerald meadow of rice awaiting harvest. On the slopes stand gabled villages of red earth and rosy brick. Many of the higher hillocks are ringed with a red circular ditch—the fortification of an ancient village site still traced in the barren grass.

This is the plateau landscape of Madagascar, where the majority of its people live. If you arrive at Antananarivo airport as an eager naturalist, babbling of lemurs and traveler's palms, people will look at you with amused tolerance, as if you landed in New York and asked, "Where are the grizzly bears?"

The plateau is only one of the diverse regions of Madagascar. When you begin to search for Madagascar's natural heritage, you will find there is no one place you can travel to see all of the species of wide-eyed lemurs, all the endemic palms, every type of rain forest orchid, or each kind of barbed succulent in the spiny desert. Instead, Madagascar's riches are scattered throughout the island, especially in the ring of natural forest types found around the coast. Bernhard Meier, the German primatologist who named the golden bamboo lemur, which was discovered only in 1986, coined the right term for Madagascar's remaining forests and forest reserves: "A necklace of pearls."

The necklace holds the treasures of Madagascar's evolution; each forest is a pearl without price. And each forest is as precious as another: They cannot be substituted for each other. Every province can boast that it has plants and animals that are unique, just as Madagascar as a whole is unique. The evolution and the conservation of Madagascar is no simple story of an island in the ocean. It is a story of "habitat islands" on a small continent, each of which you can visit as a separate pearl on the chain.

ORIGINS

Madagascar is the fourth largest island in the world, after Greenland, New Guinea, and Borneo. It is 1,600 kilometers (1,000 miles) long—the distance from London to Naples, or New York City to Orlando, Florida. Its area of 590,000 square kilometers is equal to France and Switzerland combined.

About 80 percent of Madagascar's plants and animals are endemic, that is, unique—evolved on the island and existing only there on all the earth. There are about 8,000 species of flowering plants, including up to 1,000 native orchids. Six whole plant families have evolved on Madagascar, among them the *Didiereacea*, look-alikes for giant cactuses but with woody stems like trees. There are 150 species of frogs, all endemic, some 300 species of reptiles, 90 percent endemic, and 250 breeding birds, half of them endemic. Virtually all the hundred kinds of mammals are unique, except for bats, which, like birds,

Madagascar's unique experiment in evolution began when the island separated from the supercontinent Gondwanaland between 180 and 100 million years ago. Until perhaps 40 million years ago, Madagascar could still be reached by accidental colonists floating across on rafts of vegetation, but thereafter the gap became too wide, and its flora and fauna evolved in near total isolation.

may fly in and out to Africa. I have rounded off the numbers, because we only pretend to know precisely what is there. New species are discovered every year as more and more scientists explore the forests.

Madagascar was born perhaps 175 million years ago. The continents of the Southern Hemisphere once formed a great continuous landmass, which we call Gondwanaland. As the plates of the earth's crust shifted and cracked, Australia, New Zealand, Antarctica, and South America split apart. Madagascar split from Africa where there is a dent in the coastline of present-day Kenya and Tanzania.

True oceanic islands are made of volcanic rocks, sprung from the seafloor like Hawaii or the Galapagos. Madagascar has a few (extinct) volcanoes, but it is not an ocean-born island. It is mostly composed of continental rock—ancient crystalline gneiss and granite and uplifted sediments of sandstone and limestone.

If Madagascar left Gondwanaland as far back as 175 million years ago, the split happened in the early Cretaceous era, during the age of reptiles, as flowering plants were starting to evolve. Dinosaurs apparently walked between Africa and Madagascar, but most of Madagascar's present creatures came across water.

There are still some Gondwanaland relics. The traveler's palm, *Ravenala madagascariensis,* was long the national symbol. Its nearest relatives live in South America and are descended from an ancestor that spanned the ancient continent. In 1986 John Dransfield of Kew Botanical Gardens discovered a new kind of palm tree, the "forest coconut," *Voaniala gerardii,* in the heart of the Masoala Peninsula, Madagascar's only remaining lowland rain forest. The forest coconut's only two relatives live in the Amazon and in New Zealand.

A few of the animals also date from that early period. Boa constrictors live in Madagascar and South America. They presumably once slithered across Africa, but they are extinct there now, replaced by pythons that evolved later in the old world and that seem to be more efficient occupiers of the boa's niche. *Erymnochelys,* a freshwater turtle that lies on the bottom waiting with open beak for unwary fish, is a living fossil left from Cretaceous times.

Many plants and animals arrived later, across water. Seeds were dropped by passing birds; animal emigrants floated in on logs washed out to sea on the floodwaters of African rivers. For many millions of years Madagascar was drifting southward as well as eastward, still within reach of a few hardy African colonists. All the present-day mammals are creatures that could have curled in a hollow tree—primitive mongooses and insectivores, tree mice, and ancestral lemurs.

One piece of the puzzle is the elephant bird. Until less than 500 years ago, Madagascar was home to the heaviest bird that ever lived: *Aepyornis,* which towered two and a half meters. Its thighs and shanks look more like tree trunks than bird bones. The ostrich skeleton mounted beside it in the museum of the Academie Malgache in Antananarivo seems as fragile as a ballet dancer.

It was once thought that this flightless colossus could only have reached Madagascar on foot. All large flightless birds are related: moas of New

Zealand, emus of Australia, cassowaries of South America, and the ostriches and elephant birds. The best explanation was that they originated in South America and then strode off to live in their respective corners of Gondwanaland.

New fossil discoveries have changed the picture. Now we know that the ancestors of the whole group lived in the Northern Hemisphere, and they could fly. They seem to have flown to each of the southern continents and separately evolved into the huge flightless grazers of recent times. *Aepyornis* is uniquely, wholly, a creature of Madagascar.

Geologists have proposed many ages for Madagascar, from 40 million years (which would let lemurs and *Aepyornis* cross while keeping their hands and feet dry), back to several hundred million years. Geologists are still drilling and analyzing sea sediments that may change their minds. Ornithologists changed their minds when they found new fossils—actually they excavated in old museum drawers—and suddenly understood what they saw. The jigsaw puzzle of Madagascar's origins is now reassembled in a new pattern: The island has indeed been inhabited for at least 175 million years, which explains why 80 percent of all Madagascar's plants and animals are now endemic.

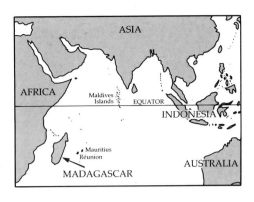

Today Madagascar lies in splendid isolation 600 kilometers off southeast Africa. Although its ecology shows clear affinities with Africa, and its culture is related to Africa as well as to Southeast Asia, there are remarkably few exchanges with either continent. This island, the fourth largest on earth, has evolved along its own enigmatic lines and is truly a world apart.

RICHES FROM POVERTY

When you land in the capital and start to look for native plants and animals, you are thus looking for the descendants of the hardy Robinson Crusoes that made it to shore in the days when Madagascar was somewhat closer to other continents. As the island drew further away, more recently evolved animals never made it at all. Madagascar has 150 species of endemic frogs, but it has no newts, salamanders, or toads. The poisonous snakes never came—they evolved too late. Half of the island's bird species are not endemic. Birds, after all, can fly back and forth, and migrants like Eleonora's falcon and broad-billed rollers do so every year. Still, Madagascar has 130 endemic species, and four or five whole endemic families of birds: the mesites, the ground rollers, the courol or cuckoo roller, the asities, and the vangas. Vangas outshine even Darwin's finches for diversity. The sicklebilled vanga gleans insects from bark; the hookbilled vanga hangs up chameleons by their necks to consume at leisure; the helmet bird is a vanga playing toucan.

Mammals are stranger still. Lemurs have radiated into the niches of monkeys and apes—but clearly because they did not confront competition with real monkeys and apes. Ancestral lemurs were once widespread in the Northern Hemisphere. They left fossils 40 to 50 million years ago in what are now Wyoming and the Paris Basin of France. They came southward to colonize Africa and then Madagascar.

Monkeys and apes appear in the African fossil record some 35 million years ago. Apparently evolution proceeds faster on the larger continents, either because a larger population has more statistical chance for change or because of more intense competition—or perhaps because of a lucky break that opened new habitat. Whatever the impetus, these new large-brained forms apparently

A sifaka's stylish bound reveals spindly but muscular limbs and clasping feet suited for an arboreal existence. Although they regularly descend to the ground to cross between trees too far apart to reach by leaping, sifaka cannot walk—only hop.

just outsmarted their lemur cousins. The surviving lemurlike animals of Africa and Asia are small, solitary, nocturnal, and insectivorous: the pottos, bush babies, and lorises, which you would never confuse with a monkey. Only on Madagascar have lemurs been free to grow large and diurnal and to live in families and social bands without interference from monkeys. Madagascar lemurs now form some 30 species, more than 40 different races. They range from the mouse lemur, small enough to sit on your thumb, to the indri, which sits two and a half feet tall and whose song carries a mile from hill to hill.

The native carnivores of Madagascar are all related to mongooses. There are no lions or leopards, no wild dogs or jackals. Like the monkeys, those modern carnivores never succeeded in crossing the channel. Instead, the largest land predator, the fossa *(Cryptoprocta ferox)*, has evolved square catlike jaws and retractile claws. Its offspring look strangely like lion cubs.

Madagascar's insectivores—the tenrecs—resemble shrews, water shrews, and hedgehogs. One, the larger spiny tenrec *(Tenrec ecaudatus)*, sets the mammalian record for the most infants in one litter—up to 34. *Hemicentetes semispinosus*, the streaked tenrec of the eastern forest, can make ultrasonic remarks by rubbing the quills on its back. Its young hear and follow their mother's calling like a little train of black-and-yellow striped pincushions.

There are seven native rodents. They are so little known it is not even clear whether they are closely related or the descendants of seven separate stocks. The largest rodent, the giant jumping rat *Hypogeomys antimena*, resembles an African springhare. It lives in one tiny area of the west, on the banks of a single stream.

This list of mammals seems strangely incomplete. Madagascar lemurs evolved to take the niches of monkeys and apes, the fossa evolved into a copycat. But where are the great herds, the grazers and browsers? For no clear reason, Madagascar's grazers were not mammals, but elephant birds and giant tortoises. They are now dead, replaced by goats and humped zebu cattle. In the forests roam wild boars, which are African bush pigs introduced by humans along with the cows and goats.

THE RAIN FOREST

As you venture forth to explore Madagascar, what do you choose first—dry forest of the west, spiny desert of the south? Perhaps you go east, where an 800-mile-long escarpment faces the trade winds and soaks in a year-round shower bath. Rain forest on the escarpment, a thousand meters above sea level, is not tall cathedral aisles with gloom at the forest floor. Here the canopy is mostly 10 to 15 meters high—wiry trees whose bare trunks are whitewashed with blotches of lichen. Enough light penetrates to encourage a tangle of bushes, lianas, tree ferns, and bamboos interlaced to form layer upon layer of habitat for small birds and mammals.

Take the train to Andasibe through the forest core. The narrow-gage track hugs the cliffs of the Mandraka gorge, wriggles like a snake in its efforts to hang on to the mountainside, and finally reaches a rift valley floor in a complete circle as though the snake were eating its tail. Below, on the escarpment's second step, live the indri.

Indri are the largest of lemurs—piebald black and white, with lemon eyes and black doglike muzzles. A group of indri look at you, then one lolls back and reaches out a languid arm to pull in a spray of leaves for its delectation. The female feeds higher in the trees than her faithful mate, while baby and its siblings, older by two- or three-year intervals, may play at hopping games.

Then they sing. The female lifts her head and howls, a broken chord of falling notes. The male chimes in a final bass note at the end of each phrase. Juveniles add their voices as the song goes on—eerie polyphony that echoes from hill to hill. From two or three kilometers away other groups answer, their thin wild wails in counterpoint to the crickets' calls and the drip of falling rain. The song of indri is the song of Madagascar, as whales sing the song of the sea.

Indri live only in the central part of the eastern rain forest. If you travel instead to Ranomafana, 200 kilometers south of Andasibe, you can see a dozen species of lemur, but not the indri. Instead, you may be lucky enough to glimpse the golden bamboo lemur or the greater bamboo lemur, Madagascar's answer to the giant panda.

Very few mammals can feed on bamboo. Three of them live in Madagascar. Two of those three are only seen in Ranomafana.

The golden bamboo lemur (*Hapalemur aures*), discovered in 1986 by Bernhard Meier and Patricia Wright, is a russet creature with golden cheeks. It scissors off the tips of Madagascar's 20-meter-tall bamboo (*Cephalostachium vigueri*), stripping and eating the pith and outer layer, which is laced with cyanide. If a human ate as much cyanide for body weight as the golden bamboo lemur, he would die three times a day.

Sharing the same forest is the greater bamboo lemur; in fact, it shares the same bamboo. Gray, tufty-eared, square-faced, it can shred the bases of the bamboo even though the plant is so tough that villagers use it for water pipes. Then there is the lesser bamboo lemur, equally gray, with big eyes and a baby face, which contents itself with nibbling bamboo leaf bases. Plant lovers may be relieved to know that Madagascar's endemic bamboos seem to have special adaptations to regenerate from all this browsing.

The three bamboo lemurs share Ranomafana's forest with nine more kinds of lemur, and a host of other wonders: suckerfooted bats, red diurnal rats, and the playful ring-tailed mongoose, as well as at least one new species of endemic fish. All these animals may be preserved, and the region as a whole find economic renaissance, through the newly declared National Park of Ranomafana.

More rain forest, for you have still hardly begun. There is the volcanic Montagne d'Ambre in the north, with its 80-meter cascades and crater lakes. There is Andohahela in the south, a rain forest fortress brooding above the spiny desert. There is the Masoala peninsula, the one remaining lowland forest on Madagascar.

On the Masoala you do find the cathedral trunks—dense straight-boled

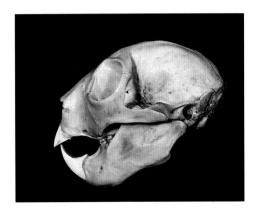

An aye aye skull shows the animal's ever growing teeth—unique among primates—which, along with the elongated, skeletal middle fingers, make this animal an oddity even among lemurs. It is classified not only as a separate species but has been given its own genus and family.

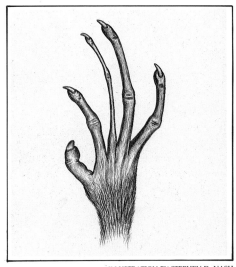

ILLUSTRATION BY STEPHEN D. NASH

Turn-of-the-century Parisians view a reconstructed skeleton of the elephant bird, the largest in a line of seven flightless birds. Madagascar's original megafauna, now extinct, included two species of giant land tortoise, like those surviving in the Galapagos Islands, a pygmy hippo, an aardvark, and several species of huge lemurs. One resembled a koala, others were more like sloths and gorillas. A giant ground-dwelling lemur was known as "tratratratra" to Malagasy, who described it to 17th-century naturalist Etienne de Flacourt.

precious hardwoods. The land rises almost sheer, at slopes up to 70 degrees and more, straight out of the Bay of Antongil. In this roadless jungle live the forest coconut and also the newly found red lemur palm (*Lemurophoenix hallouxi*). The rain forest canopy, 20 to 30 meters above, is packed with orchids, ferns, and other epiphytes. White-fronted lemurs hang over you from the lianas—the female gray-brown with white "surprised" eyebrows, the male with a fuzzy white mane on head and chest. They click-grunt their alarm, tails swinging like pendulums in time to the call, then bound away—an infant clinging like a moneybelt around the female's waist. But if you wake in the morning in this forest, you hear a different call, a bellowing roar that echoes along the hillside. This is the red-ruffed lemur's morning challenge.

Red-ruffs are one of Madagascar's most beautiful lemurs: gleaming russet fur, black faces, and plumed black tails. They have twins or triplets that they raise in leafy nests, unlike the other large diurnal lemurs. And they live only on the Masoala peninsula.

The strangest of all the lemurs is one of the very few not confined only to one of the pearls. The aye aye of Madagascar is a patchwork animal with bat ears, beaver teeth, and a skeletal middle finger on each hand. It strips open coconuts or tree bark with those teeth and uses the strange finger as tactile organ, probe, and spoon to extract coconut meat or the pulped remains of a burrowing insect.

The aye aye has an ecological niche like no other; or rather, a niche that has elements of woodpecker, squirrel, and raccoon, none of which lives on Madagascar. Perhaps because it has so little competition, it may have lived throughout Madagascar's forest in historic times. Now, though, your best hope of seeing it is in Mananara, on the mainland side of the Bay of Antongil, across from the Masoala peninsula. In most places, this strange creature has provoked fear and horror, and according to taboos it must be killed on sight. But in Mananara it is the opposite—aye ayes must be protected in spite of their raids on the coconuts, and if you kill one by accident, you should bury it with prayers. In the end this ancient belief may help the people in turn: A UNESCO–funded biosphere reserve has been declared in the area.

THE SPINY DESERT

In the spiny desert of Madagascar, not just 80 percent but 95 percent of all plants are endemic. Didiereaceae dominate the landscape, their cactuslike fingers silhouetted against the sky. Twisted euphoria drip latex that can sear the skin and blind the eye.

There is life among the thorns of this shadeless land. Bands of white sifaka richochet through the trees, carrying their babies on their backs. Radiated tortoises trundle over leaf litter. Thorny-tailed iguanid lizards and zoonosaurus lizards with a dark pigment spot over their "third eye" bask on rocks. And always there are humped zebu cattle, pride of Antandroy pastoralists. Even here there are separate centers of evolution—separate pearls.

In the southeast, on the inland side of the eastern mountains, a "rainfall fault line" marks a shift within a few kilometers from 350 centimeters of rain annually down to 50 centimeters. In that area the spiny desert grows on the same granite that underlies the eastern mountains. The rock is waterproof, so there is a fairly high water table. There is a baobab species, *Adansonia za*, confined to that region—the largest baobab in girth of Madagascar's seven species. The giant ultra-rare *Aloe suzannae* grows three meters tall and is topped by two-meter spikes of lemon-yellow flowers. The octopus tree, *Didierea trollii*, whose branches first grow vertically and then turn horizontally, is also confined to small patches of the southeastern zone.

In the southwest near Tulear the desert flora grow on chalky limestone. Granite holds water, but the western limestone lets it drain away. The plants here are not only seared by the sky but parched at their roots.

Much of the southwestern region holds only low scrubby bushes. Where there is forest, *Alluaudia comosa* funnels out of the ground like a thorny vegetable tornado. *Didierea madagascariensis*, defended by its crucifixes of spines, replaces the tall finger-trees of the southeast. The portly baobab of the southeast gives way to the dwarf baobab, *Adamsonia fony*, a bottle-shaped cylinder some three to six meters tall, pinched in at the top and surmounted by a few branches that seem to be twisted together out of coat hangers.

A few animals are also confined to just one part of the desert. The long-tailed ground roller, *Uratelornis*, lives in just one small area north of Tulear, where birdwatchers travel from Europe and America to find it.

Hidden within the desert, a lemur-jump away from the forest of thorns, are even richer pearls. The few well-watered regions, gallery forests by rivers, are covered with tamarind and acacia trees: Berenty in the east, Sept Lacs and Beza-Mahafaly in the west.

It is there that ring-tailed lemurs promenade in troops of ten or twenty, their striped question-mark tails above their backs. It is there that flying foxes (*Pteropus rufus*) roost—rufus-furred bats with a meter-wide wing span that wheel against the sky. And it is there that predators nest—the Madagascar buzzard (*Buteo madagascariensis*) and the Madagascar harrier hawk (*Gymnogenys madagascariensis*). Where prey is rich, raptors can live well.

These places, now under intense threat, were always isolated pearls, the promised lands where water flows through the spiny south.

THE DRY FOREST

The baobab forest, north of Morondava, is dry for nine months of the year. Trees lose their leaves and stand bare in a winter of heat and drought. Then, as the first rains of spring drench the baobabs, emerald vangas sing, and swallow-tailed butterflies congregate around the puddles.

Giant jumping rats emerge from hibernation to demolish sprouting tree seedlings. *Pyxis planicauda*, the flat-tailed tortoise, shuffles through leaf litter left from the winter. That little tortoise and the giant jumping rat are confined to just one small river basin in the baobab forest. Perhaps "river" is a misnomer. For most of the year the Kirindy River is only a narrow bed of dry sand, but when the rains come, it can turn into a shallow flood kilometers wide on the flat land around. The rich soil left by the flood supports this pearl.

Madagascar's tenrecs, an endemic family of insectivores, have been called "the closest living things to the very first mammals that evolved on earth." They combine a primitive body plan with unique specializations that make them scientific treasures. Streaked tenrecs (Hemicentetes semispinosus) have been observed to communicate using high frequency sounds created by rubbing their quills together. This species is listed in the Guinness Book of World Records *as having the shortest maturation time of any mammal—only 35 days from birth to sexual maturity. Semispinosus lives in multigenerational groups of up to 20 individuals—one aspect of their social lives that has evoked parallels with elephants. Their tiny eyes inspired a Malagasy proverb, "If you don't see much, you won't need much."*

Named after its discoverer, Malagasy naturalist André Peyrieras, the world's smallest chameleon, (Brookesia peyrieresi), *here adult size, is perfectly camouflaged for an existence on forest floors in the northeast. Many Malagasy are frightened of chameleons and are particularly repelled by the diminutive* Brookesia *species, of which it is said in some regions that whoever harms one can expect great misfortune.*

Hardier animals, which survive elsewhere, also congregate here: Red-fronted lemurs drink in pools, and fossa stalks the lemurs. Five small nocturnal lemurs coexist here, weathering the winter drought with diverse strategies, including outright hibernation. Along with the mouse lemur, the dwarf lemur *(Cheirogaleus medius)* is the only hibernating primate. It survives for about eight months on the stored fat in its tail.

The dry forests extend in scattered pockets up to the far north of the island. Ankarafantsika has black-headed brown lemurs *(Lemur fulvus fulvus)* and Coquerel's sifaka *(Propithecus verreauxi coquerel)* with maroon eagle-wing marks on its arms and legs. Farther north, on the enchanted islands of Nosy Be and Nosy Komba, live *Lemur macaco*—black males and golden females with sunbursts of whiskers round their heads. Farther still, on the mainland, black males and golden females have smooth crew cuts and blue-green eyes *(Lemur flavifrons)*. In the far north, as the circle closes again to reach the rain forest, you may see crowned lemurs *(Lemur coronatus)*, the female reddish, the male a svelte pale gray with an orange V-shaped tiara. Of course, with each of these changes of lemur species you find a new community of plants, lizards, and insects.

ISLANDS OF STONE

Within the dry forest lies perhaps the most spectacular of all Madagascar's habitats. Just as the pearls of gallery forest lie hidden within the desert, so in the dry forest are hidden the *tsingy.*

Tsingy comes from the Malagasy verb "to tiptoe." The karst pinnacles of the tsingy rise so close together that the Malagasy say there is no room to plant your foot.

Over millions of years rainfall has worn the limestone of the tsingy into sharp pinnacles. Floods of wetter epochs hollowed out caves.

The tsingy of Bemaraha—150 square kilometers of needles up to 20 meters high—is interlaced by trees where snow-white Deckens' sifaka *(Propithecus verreaux deckeni)*, red-fronted lemurs *(fulvus rufus)*, and forked lemurs *(Phaner furcifer)* live in hanging gardens in the sky.

The tsingy of Ankarana in the north shelters crowned lemurs which teeter along the rock points between secret forests hidden among the stones. Under the Ankarana, crocodiles lurk in sunless caverns. And along the high-water line of ancient floods lie the skulls of greater bamboo lemurs. Alongside them are skulls of a sloth-like lemur with arms as long as a man's *(Paleoproprithecus maximus)* and a cow-face lemur as large as a female gorilla *(Megaladapis edwardsi)*. These giants did not find a sanctuary where they could survive and so died out sometime in the past thousand years.

These lemurs lost the confrontation with humankind. Madagascar has already seen the end of its megafauna—the giant lemurs, the great land tortoises, the elephant birds. What is left are small animals that live in the jungle on steep mountains, or in desert too dry to farm, or hide in secret forests and dark caves among the pinnacles.

The Malagasy know that what they have lost is gone forever. They know, also, how precious are the pearls that remain today.

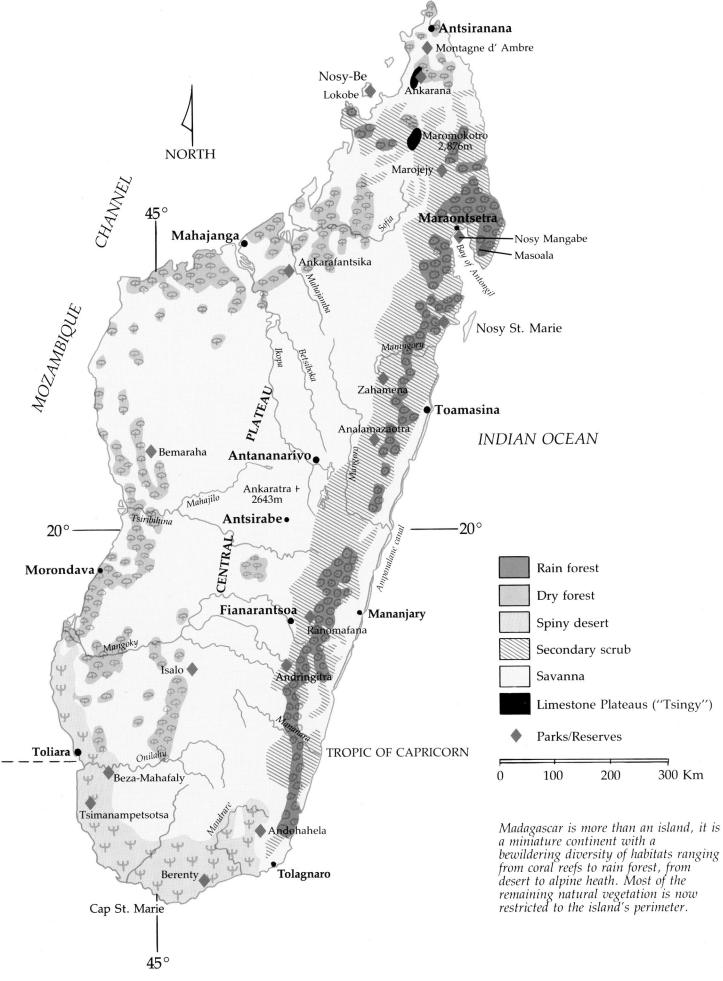

NORTH

CHANNEL

MOZAMBIQUE

45°

Antsiranana

Montagne d' Ambre

Nosy-Be
Lokobe

Ankarana

Maromokotro
2,876m

Marojejy

Mahajanga

Ankarafantsika

Sofia

Maraontsetra

Nosy Mangabe

Masoala

Bay of Antongil

Nosy St. Marie

Maningory

Mahajamba

Ikopa

Betsiboka

PLATEAU

Zahamena

Analamazaotra

Toamasina

Bemaraha

Antananarivo

Ankaratra ⊢
2643m

INDIAN OCEAN

Mahajilo

Tsiribihina

20°

Antsirabe

20°

Mangoro

Morondava

CENTRAL

Fianarantsoa

Ranomafana

Mananjary

Mangoky

Isalo

Andringitra

Ampanalane canal

Toliara

Onilahy

Mananara

TROPIC OF CAPRICORN

Beza-Mahafaly

Tsimanampetsotsa

Mandrare

Andohahela

Berenty

Tolagnaro

Cap St. Marie

45°

	Rain forest
	Dry forest
	Spiny desert
	Secondary scrub
	Savanna
	Limestone Plateaus ("Tsingy")
◆	Parks/Reserves

0   100   200   300 Km

*Madagascar is more than an island, it is
a miniature continent with a
bewildering diversity of habitats ranging
from coral reefs to rain forest, from
desert to alpine heath. Most of the
remaining natural vegetation is now
restricted to the island's perimeter.*

37

LAND
OF
BAOBABS

Baobabs such as Adansonia *dominate the dry forests of the west. Their great age—they are known to live for thousands of years—and great utility—their bark is used to thatch roofs, twine rope, and cure ills—inspired their Malagasy name "Reniala," meaning "Mother of the Forest." To many older people, certain baobabs are places of spiritual power, and offerings are made at their base.*

Fossa (Cryptoprocta ferox), left, the largest land predator in Madagascar, is widespread but seldom seen. Its lineage is ancient, dating from a time many millions of years ago when cats and dogs, the main evolutionary lines of today's predators, did not yet exist. Taxonomically a huge cousin of the mongoose but by life-style a small, powerful panther the size of a large dog, fossa (pronounced "foosh") ranges from rain forest to desert. It is most often glimpsed in the dry forests of the west, where it hunts birds and small mammals in trees and on the ground. A troop of red-fronted brown lemurs (Lemur fulvus rufus), *right, drink nervously from a water hole where the scent of a fossa that preceded them still lingers. Sakalava people near Morondava claim that fossa attack livestock and occasionally even humans during fossa mating season, when males lose their habitual wariness. They say fossa sometimes raises its young in the crown of a baobab and carries water to them in the cup of its curled tail.*

AN EMERALD WORLD

*A cascade of orchids (*Angraecum sp.*) attached to a fallen tree in the Ranomafana forest represents but one of a thousand orchid species— more than are found in all of Africa—native to the Great Red Island. Madagascar's 8,000 flowering plants account for 25 percent of the entire African flora, even though the island makes up only 2 percent of Africa's landmass. Much of this floral wealth grows in the remaining rain forests of the east, where discoveries are still being made.*

Known as "taha fisaka" to locals, **Uroplatus fimbriatus** *to scientists, the leaf-tailed gecko, left, is endemic, as are 95 percent of all Malagasy reptiles. This nocturnal denizen of the eastern rain forest sports claws on sucker feet, has eyes with four pupils each, and can change color like a chameleon.* **Phelsuma madagascariensis,** *above, a colorful diurnal gecko here silhouetted on a banana leaf, is in great demand among European reptile-lovers, who buy many of the animals exported from Madagascar.*

A ring-tailed mongoose (Galidia elegans), one of only seven indigenous carnivores, pauses before disappearing into the underbrush of the Ranomafana rain forest.

A symbol of all that's weird, wonderful, and ill-understood about Madagascar, aye aye (Daubentonia madagascariensis) *qualifies as one of the strangest mammals on earth. This cat-size, aberrant lemur with leathery bat ears, staring owl eyes, bushy fox tail, ever growing rodent teeth, and skeletal fingers has such a ghostly appearance that it has earned a place in folklore as a harbinger of death. Some older Malagasy are afraid to even speak its name, which they pronounce "eh eh." Aye aye fills the ecological niche of a woodpecker, a bird not found in Madagascar, for it uses its unusual teeth and fingers to pry for grubs under tree bark (right). But farmers know that aye aye is equally well equipped to raid their coconut crops. After chiseling through the hard outer husk, aye aye uses its spindly fingers to scoop out the tender coconut flesh through a tiny hole in the nut (left). Until recently, aye aye was believed to be nearly extinct and restricted to rain forests of the northeast, but since photographer Frans Lanting's documentation of aye aye presence in western Madagascar in 1985, numerous sightings from other regions indicate that the creature is more widespread than previously thought.*

Microcebus murinus, *the mouse lemur (above), is indeed only the size of a mouse. At fifty grams it is the smallest primate on earth. It along with the dwarf lemur are the only primates capable of hibernation. Indri* (Indri indri), *right, is the largest surviving lemur. Rain forests inhabited by these arboreal teddy bears resound every morning with their undulating choral chants, which waft over the hills like polyphonic saxophones, drawing response from neighboring colonies until the whole forest reverberates with their eerie harmonies. No one has yet succeeded in keeping indri alive in captivity, perhaps because its diet in the wild includes over 50 species of plants. Villagers know indri as ''babakoto,'' meaning ''cousin to man,'' and many still abide by the taboo against killing it.*

Displaying a gymnast's grace and an archer's precision, a young Parson's chameleon (Chameleo parsonii) stuns a grasshopper with his body-length tongue, an extraordinary muscular organ with a sticky tip.

ISLANDS
OF
STONE

Domain of succulent plants such as Kalanchoa gastonisboniri, *the limestone plateaus of Madagascar's west remain one of its most inaccessible regions.*

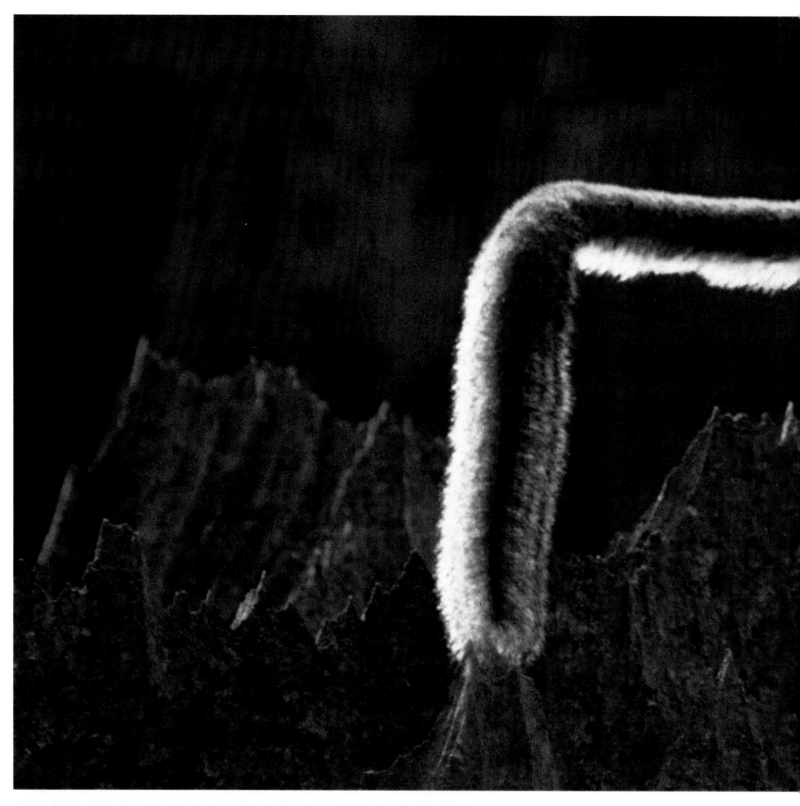

Few Westerners have had a chance to explore the Tsingy de Bemaraha (left), a plateau of karst topography in the west, where the eroding action of wind and water has carved a fantastic labyrinth of razor-sharp pinnacles up to 20 meters high. Under French colonial

administration, some 150,000
hectares of this extraordinary
landscape were proclaimed a nature
reserve, Madagascar's largest, but it
remained practically unknown to the
outside world until Lanting gained
access to it in recent years and
publicized its existence. In the north
the limestone massif of Ankarana,

where a crowned lemur (Lemur
coronatus) balances nimbly on
stone spires, is also protected
as a reserve.

OVERLEAF

Underneath the spectacular scenery
of the Ankarana massif lies a maze
of more than 100 kilometers of caves
and passages that open up into
dramatic gorges and isolated forests.
The largest known cave in the
Ankarana massif, Andriafabe,
dwarfs two explorers.

FORGOTTEN
SHORES

Flamingos (Phoenicopterus ruber) *stretch across a coastal lagoon near the mouth of the Tsiribihina River. While much of the current attention of scientists and conservationists goes to Madagascar's unique forests, its coastal treasures remain largely unexplored. Other than the fact that flamingos return to nesting sites at Lac Tsimanampetsotsa, the movements of these birds in their thousands are still uncharted.*

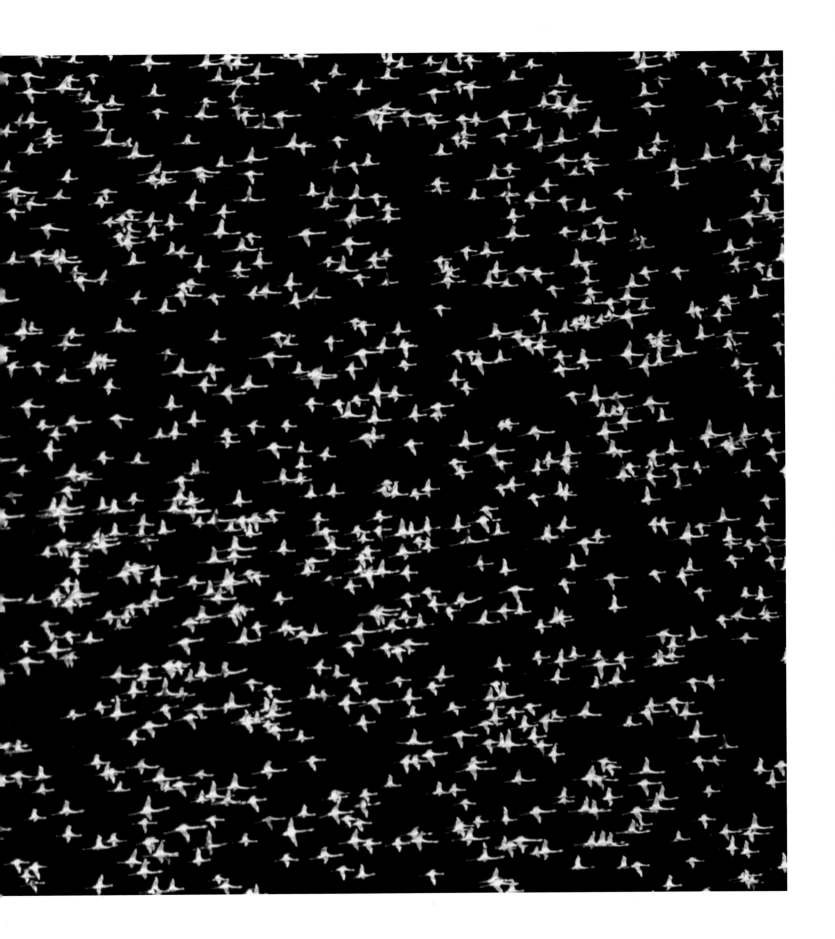

Madagascar's 5,000 kilometers of coastline mirror the diversity of its interior. Bordering on the Mozambique Channel in the west are coral reefs backed by sandy beaches as well as muddy mangrove swamps of great importance to migratory shore birds (left). On the humid east coast, land drops steeply into the depths of the Indian Ocean. Great baleen whales, humpbacks and blues, cruise into the sheltered Bay of Antongil, where a few remaining dugongs lull in shallows, and the nearly unbroken rain forest of the Masoala peninsula still comes down to the sea's edge.

A
JUNGLE
OF
THORNS

The arid southern bush is as otherworldly as it appears: Ninety-five percent of all plants that thrive here are found nowhere else on earth, not even in other parts of Madagascar. Among the striking sights of this spiny desert are the twisted tentacles of Didierae trollii, *sometimes called the octopus tree, which resembles a cactus but is not. Rather, it is one of the many astonishing examples Madagascar provides of convergent evolution, the principle that lifeforms different in origin may end up looking or acting alike when faced with similar conditions over long periods of time.*

Arid by nature and prone to periodic droughts, the southern bush has given rise to water-storing plants of various forms. Pachypodiums, *at left a species called bottle tree, and aloes at right, plant families represented in Madagascar by many species, swell up visibly after rains.*

With a baby holding on for dear life, a ring-tailed lemur (Lemur catta) known as "maki" streaks across the red sand of Berenty.

Ringtails, the most terrestrial and best known of all lemurs, turn to sunbathing on chilly winter mornings (left), a habit that has earned them a reputation as sun worshippers among Malagasy, for whom the east, the direction of the rising sun, is of great spiritual importance. A ringtail baby inspects a tamarind seed pod picked up by its mother in Berenty, a private nature reserve (below).

*All lemurs leap, but none do it with the grace of sifaka (*Propithecus verreauxi)*, the white acrobat of the arid south. Named for its alarm call, emitted as a hissed "sefaakh," this gibbonlike lemur can cover eight meters in one jump. After kicking off with powerful hind legs, sifaka turns in midair to grab another tree feet first.*

THE WAYS OF THE ANCESTORS

John Mack

Avy tsy nangeha nasesiky ny raza.

The ancestors come into our lives like guests who need no invitation.

MALAGASY SAYING

Even on market day life unfolds at a medieval pace in a highland village near Ambalamanarana, where strong traditions and economic stagnation are deterrents to change. Underneath the apparent simplicity of rural Malagasy lies a complex cosmology that governs every facet of their lives.

I met Rakotoarivo twice. To understand him is to understand the dilemma of modern Madagascar. The first time was toward dusk on a fine warm day nearing the end of September, early spring in Madagascar. His son and I had been traveling back from the island's east coast, where we had spent several months studying the traditional life of the peoples of the rain forests. Now the hot humidity of the coast was gradually changing to a drier, more pleasant climate. The oppressive forests were giving way to open woodland. In front of us a series of steep escarpments remained to be climbed before we reached the high treeless plateau at the center of the island. My friend's home village was an obvious place for us to spend the night.

As we approached, thin columns of smoke were rising from the surrounding bush. At their base we found Rakotoarivo supervising operations. He was, people said, a champion of *tavy*, the local word for the practice of slash-and-burn agriculture. He, unlike some others, was careful to ensure that the fires were dampened down so the flames would not spread untended overnight. Tavy is the annual prelude to planting rice. It also, however, depletes the land, and large tracts of forest have now become barren. When we arrived in Antananarivo the following day, a haze hung over the capital. That, people assured me, was smoke blown up from the fires in the eastern forest. It happened like this every spring, they said.

Four years later in 1989, I met Rakotoarivo again in the same rice fields. This time he was standing on top of an open tomb, proudly holding the national flag of Madagascar. Unlike tavy, the event I witnessed this time had official approval. From his vantage point Rakotoarivo surveyed a large crowd of relatives wheeling excitedly around the solid stone family grave. They carried aloft the heavily wrapped remains of, among others, his own brother, who had died some ten years previously. *Famadihana*, the name of the ceremony, involved rewrapping the bones of relatives. At the head of the procession of shrouded remains, formal framed photographs of the deceased were displayed. The atmosphere was not morbid but joyous, celebratory.

Rakotoarivo is a peasant farmer, as are many of the people of Madagascar, the Malagasy. He is literate. And he is Christian—indeed, under his guidance the famadihana had been punctuated with prayers. He is an ordinary man with simple tastes and limited means. Yet he and others like him are often portrayed as villains, wasting economic and environmental resources. Tavy persists though officially discouraged; famadihana has increased dramatically since the beginning of the 20th century. Some missionaries frown at its popularity. Rakotoarivo could easily be made to seem both an irresponsible fire-raiser and a morbid resurrectionist. But he is neither. He is as much a victim as a villain, obliged to survive in an environment he is unwittingly depleting of resources. The reburial ceremonies he conducts are part of his attempt to make sense of the modern world.

Watching Rakotoarivo take charge at two different occasions, I came to realize that the events he oversaw were not completely separate. He himself certainly saw them as linked.

DISTRIBUTION
OF HOMELANDS

One nation united by language and culture, Madagascar's 11 million people nonetheless form a diverse society. Strong tribal affiliations stem from ethnic differences as well as old political boundaries separating former kingdoms. Tribes include the Merina (meaning "People-of-the-Highlands"), the most numerous and politically dominant group; the Betsimisaraka, ("The Many-United"), whose name goes back to an east coast empire founded by Ratsimilaho, the Malagasy son of an English pirate; the Antandroy ("People-of-the-Thorns"), a dark-skinned pastoralist people from the southern desert; and the Sakalava ("People-of-the-Long-Valleys"), formerly ruled by their own royalty, now a people who reckon their riches in cattle. Among Sakalava, "tromba," possession by spirits, is quite common. Mikea and Vezo are considered separate clans within the Sakalava tribe.

In the West we automatically think of agricultural practice in economic terms, as a means of subsistence. Burial rites are an aspect of religious belief. When we talk loosely of "ancestor worship" in Madagascar, our very language endorses this view. Conservation, interest in the future of the island's environment, has generally concerned itself with tavy and related practices; it strives for better economic management and tries to make agriculture less wasteful of natural resources. Famadihana has not seemed relevant. But ideas of fertility and well-being are involved in both tavy and famadihana. In Malagasy thought, economic and moral welfare both derive from the same mystical source, summed up in the broad term *razana*, "the ancestors."

Razana are first of all something physical. They are the skeletal remains of relatives gathered together in the family tomb. Every Malagasy has the ambition to one day join the company of the razana. For the living, death is not an extinction—it is a change of address, an elevation to another level of existence. The ultimate sanction for serious misdeeds is not death itself but the threat that your family may exclude your remains from burial in the ancestral tomb. Your bones properly incorporated in the right resting place are your guarantee of "living on."

The ancestors, however, are also a metaphysical concept. They are an imposing point of reference. The vitality of the living is seen as derived from the ancestors. Their blessings are the source of human well-being. Rewrapping your own deceased relatives, attending to their potential needs in the course of famadihana, is a way of celebrating the promotion of the recently dead to the status of razana. And it is also a means of ensuring their benevolent interest in you, their descendants. Rakotoarivo had all this in mind when he turned the bones of his brother.

Outsiders might think that such ideas are an inheritance of less educated, rural communities living lives encased by tradition. But we completely misunderstand the importance of the ancestors for Malagasy if we see them as some arcane piece of cultural baggage slowing down the inevitable march of progress. To Malagasy, the ancestors are a part of development and progress rather than an impediment to them.

Ceremonies associated with the ancestors are by no means the preserve of remote communities. Famadihana take place on the very outskirts of the capital. Here the organizers are not necessarily the urban poor, but businessmen, doctors, public servants, and university teachers. The ancestors remain a vital point of reference for all Malagasy. And if that is the case, then development and conservation strategies should certainly take them into account.

TOMBS

These points struck me most forcibly when traveling for the first time to southern Madagascar. Tombs along the route show considerable variation in traditional form and construction. Sometimes they are decorated. In the south, wood sculpture known as *aloalo* is often placed on top. Sometimes they are plain cut-stone vaults, as in the center of the island, the region of Imerina.

Older tombs are easily distinguishable from newer ones. The most recent are clad in cement, painted white, and decorated with colored designs—flowers or geometric patterns or lively scenes from daily life. Illustrations of local stories featuring crocodiles are very popular.

According to a popular Malagasy saying, a house is only for a lifetime, a tomb is for eternity. This contrast is still obvious in places where tombs are solid stone structures but huts are made of wood or reed. In central Madagascar, however, a change has taken place. Once, it was forbidden to use any material other than wood for building houses. Antananarivo was constructed entirely from planks. Because it stands in the midst of a treeless expanse, the planks had to be transported long distances. In the mid-19th century, however, missionaries introduced techniques for making mud bricks, and the whole architecture of central Madagascar slowly changed. The contrast in solidity between tombs and houses began to disappear.

The current trend toward construction of new and more ostentatious tombs tips the balance again. Outside, tombs are decorated in ways that houses are not. Inside, I have seen a tomb decorated with expensive lace curtains not found in any house in the nearby village.

Malagasy treat the dead as living, right down to the details of the furnishings in their abode. Standing on his family tomb several days before the rewrapping ceremony, Rakotoarivo addressed each of the deceased who were to be taken from the tomb. "Rakotobe, my brother, don't go to the market next Friday. We will be coming for your famadihana. Mother, we know you like to keep an eye on things, but don't go to inspect the early shoots of rice in the fields." And when the bodies were brought from the tomb to be reshrouded, they were given a present they enjoyed in life—chewing tobacco, a small tot of rum. The ancestors were also told of all the advances that had taken place since their demise. "Look," Rakotoarivo said, "we have put a new corrugated iron roof on the church. A new road is being built that is already up to the outskirts of the village. Soon we will have a taxi to take us to town."

The ancestors do not anchor Malagasy to unalterable ways. They give continuity and direction in a changing world. The idea of the ancestors provides a model of change.

PROFILE: THE PEOPLE OF MADAGASCAR

Madagascar in its relatively brief history has already been the scene of immense cultural changes. Those who settled the island have forfeited their ancestry, even if they have all come to believe in the importance of the ancestors. Unraveling Malagasy history is not unlike trying to solve a mystery novel set at a weekend party in a remote country house. Whatever the backgrounds of the arriving guests, the chemistry of their interaction has set them upon a mutual adventure. They have available to them only the experiences derived from their varied backgrounds and the immediate resources offered by their new surroundings. In the end everyone's life is changed by the events that take place. It is not an overstatement to say that, as it has been reworked and remolded throughout history, Malagasy culture has emerged as unique.

A folded palm or "ravenala" leaf becomes a rice spoon in the hands of a Malagasy displaying his people's ingenuity at using materials from the natural world as alternatives for store-bought products.

Initial impressions of a foreign culture are not a reliable guide to its origin. Those of the traveler arriving at Ivato, the island's international airport, are frankly bewildering. Conversations overheard are in the soft mellifluous Malagasy tongue spoken throughout the island. It is a language in love with syllables, which, as I know from my own stumbling attempts to learn it, makes it somewhat impenetrable to the beginner. It is also full of proverbial sayings and colorful figures of speech. Travelers familiar with Swahili, the common language of East Africa, will be at no special advantage in following what is said. Malagasy is not African in origin. Rather, its affinities are with Malayo-Polynesian speech from the other side of the Indian Ocean.

The physical features of many of the faces at the airport concourse also betray a Southeast Asia connection. As recently as A.D. 500 migrants with an ultimate origin somewhere in the Indonesian/Malaysian world began to settle the island. According to most reliable sources, they had skirted around the northern fringes of the Indian Ocean, bringing with them their distinctive outrigger sailing canoes, their language, music, and other aspects of their culture. Some commentators have proposed the idea of a trip directly across the open vastness of the ocean as the means by which the island was peopled. (Such a voyage has been successfully recreated in recent years.) But the fact that intervening islands, such as Mauritius, were unoccupied at the time of their discovery by Europeans in the early 16th century makes this a very unlikely scenario.

However they may have arrived, the initial settlers were fishermen who seldom ventured inland, content to exploit the bounty of the sea. But within a few centuries large cattle camps were established in southern Madagascar, giving that area the economic balance it retains today. The development of an Arab-Swahili trading network along the reaches of the western Indian Ocean at the end of the first millennium A.D. stretched as far as Madagascar and provided a vehicle for the spread of Islamic communities. By the 13th century mosques had been constructed on the island's northern shores. A unique Arab script is still used by native scholars in the southeast of the island. Islam itself, however, petered out. Today's Malagasy Muslims arrived from the Indian subcontinent in the 19th century.

Africa has played a role, albeit limited, in Malagasy history. The early cattle-keeping communities in the south were possibly of African origin. African influence, however, has left few distinctive traces—little input into the Malagasy language, for instance, and none of the round huts that characterize the native architecture of the nearby continent. Yet just as the natural history of Madagascar is a unique treasure, its cultural history represents a special blend of Indian Ocean peoples, including those from Africa.

The most persuasive evidence against trying to carve up Malagasy life into constituent parts and track their separate derivations is reflected in the Vezo. These people of the sandy west coast live a life that is in some respects closest to that of the island's original inhabitants. Vezo have contact with inland peoples, but their own economic niche is the exploitation of the resources of sea and coastline. Some of their activities seem to mirror the cultures of the

Proclaimed king in 1787, Ramboasalama took the new name "Andrianampoinimerina-ndriantsimitoviaminandriampanjaka," for convenience shortened to "Andrianampoinimerina." This most famous of Merina monarchs extended his kingdom by conquest and consolidated the structure of Malagasy society by enlightened administration. He organized the "fokonolona," the traditional council of village elders that to this day plays an important part in local decision making.

interior but have been adapted to their own environment. Elsewhere in Madagascar, for instance, the sacrifice of cattle and the displaying of their skulls on poles and tombs is widespread. It can be argued that the Vezo practice of sacrificing turtles and the subsequent display of their remains is a maritime version of the same ritual.

In other ways the Vezo are distinctly different. For example, they do not practice male circumcision. That would be heresy for the vast majority of Malagasy, a reason for not burying someone in the family tomb. The most typically Malayo-Polynesian people in one respect turn out to be the least typically Malagasy. The lesson is that Malagasy culture is more than a mere amalgam of its parts.

RICE

Possibly the most famous statement in Malagasy history came from Andrianampoinimerina, the unifying ruler of the Merina kingdom, which held sway in the island's interior during the 19th century. "The seas," he said from the fastness of central Madagascar, "are the limits of my rice fields." The rice fields became a metaphor for the kingdom itself. Rakotoarivo's immediate forebears lay in the way of the expanding kingdom. They, like many others, succumbed to Merina domination. This is why the Bezanozano today practice both tavy, the agricultural practice of the forest peoples, and famahidana, an inheritance from the Merina.

Rice itself, as emblematic as it now is of Malagasy cuisine, has only been grown in recent centuries. It did not arrive with the early settlers. Over time, the ancestors seem to have been amenable to major innovations.

Andrianampoinimerina is credited with another famous statement. "Rice and I," he said, "are one." Nowadays if you look around Imerina, the plains immediately beyond the capital, one meaning of this remark is obvious. They are one enormous rice paddy, with villages standing above the outcrops like islands in a sea. Many villages are linked only by dikes, constructed in part from earth removed as canals were built to ensure maximum irrigation. That vast engineering feat, which transformed the landscape, was a remarkable initiative of the founder of the Merina kingdom.

Linking the identity of rice with the person of Andrianampoinimerina has another important implication. Today in much of Madagascar no meal without rice is regarded as complete. By comparison, what is eaten with rice is seen as relatively unimportant.

Andrianampoinimerina's various statements about rice are not quoted or remembered simply to cite precedent for a gargantuan appetite. He, after all, was no ordinary mortal. He was the kingdom's single most important ritual and religious figure, emerging finally as a divine ruler. Equating rice to himself established it in some sense as a sacred substance. Rice production thus became more than mere subsistence labor: It was also a sacred duty.

Now, well over a century later, there is no Merina monarchy. Yet rice remains more than a mundane necessity of life. For Rakotoarivo, rice is the measure of all things. The traditional Malagasy calendar is constructed in terms

The governor of Betafo poses in Western attire around the turn of the century. After settlement attempts by Portuguese, British, Dutch, and pirates of many nations, the French finally managed to subject Madagascar to colonial rule in 1896. The Merina monarchy was abolished and French culture forcefully superimposed on the Malagasy way of life, a development that strongly influences Madagascar to this day. Children in school were taught in French about French subjects and learned practically nothing about their own unique homeland. A popular revolt in 1947 was repressed by French troops at a cost of tens of thousands of Malagasy lives. Independence came in name in 1960, but not until the nationalist revolution of 1972 did Madagascar achieve a significant break with its colonial past.

By undoing her hair from the typical close-cropped braids, a Merina woman gives expression to her grief over a death. Painting by Malagasy artist Rainimaharosoa.

of the different stages in the cultivation of rice. Malagasy vocabulary clusters around rice, as that of the Inuit of the Arctic clusters around the condition of snow. Rice and its attributes are the basis of innumerable sayings. I once asked Rakotoarivo how far it was to a neighboring village. His answer was the number of pots of rice that could be cooked in the span it took to walk there. Rice preparation is an ancestral measure of time.

Rice fields represent the toil of the razana. Working them, maintaining them, assures the crucial continuity of the living with the ancestors. The ancestors are addressed at the beginning of work in the fields. Some token, often a sprinkle of rum, is poured in their honor. They are part of the whole procedure, and their beneficial influence is required for success.

LEMURS, CROCODILES, AND CATTLE

Apart from agriculture, Malagasy make use of the environment in a range of other ways. The forests are home to a whole spectrum of plants that are the basis of traditional medicine. At the famadihana Rakotoarivo's nephew was stung by a scorpion, an alarming event. A clinic was not far away. I suggested taking him there. The victim, however, preferred a local healer and his stock of medicines derived from the forest. A concoction was quickly prepared using scrapings from various roots, and an invocation to the ancestors was spoken to empower the remedy. The patient recovered rapidly. Everyone present agreed that hospitals, even if stocked with modern pharmaceuticals, could not achieve this. The loss of these natural resources and the traditional knowledge that goes with them would be a tragedy.

The animals of the forest are rather less valued locally than its flora. Environmentalists have drawn consolation from the report that the *babakoto,* or indri, the largest of the lemurs, is respected as a cousin by the Betsimisaraka people. Its privileged position derives from a belief that the souls of dead people pass through it before they settle into the tomb.

Certainly lemurs are not systematically hunted, though traps are often laid to try and catch them. (The wild boar is the only large animal consistently hunted.) In some villages I have seen lemurs kept on long chains like pets. But there is no general belief that the spirits of the dead migrate into lemurs, and indeed no very clear idea about the separation of flesh and soul. The emphasis in burial procedures, in fact, is on the significance and interpretation of the physical changes that happen to the body.

This is not to say that individuals may not conceive a particular respect for certain animals. I once stayed in an Antaimoro village in the southeast, where a number of families had adopted a taboo against disturbing tenrecs. As a result everyone would wake up in the morning to a room bristling with the hedgehoglike creatures!

Perhaps the only animal to have a consistent symbolic status for Malagasy is the crocodile. As the island's only dangerous carnivore, it fills a role similar to the leopard in many African societies, acting as a metaphor for power, both human and mystical. Crocodile teeth are regarded as powerful protective devices and are often worn around the neck. In the 19th century Merina aristocracy constructed elaborate talismans with silver and gold imitations of crocodile teeth. Hats sometimes sported real teeth around the base.

The crocodile is also seen as an agent of the ancestors. I recall a tragic incident in which a helpless young man had been killed by a crocodile near his home, in sight of friends and relatives. People falling into rivers are sometimes expected to find their own way to the shore, not because potential rescuers want to protect their own lives but because the "accident" may have been willed by the ancestors. The dangers of interfering with ancestral intention are as much a deterrent to mounting a rescue attempt as are the chances of encountering a hostile crocodile.

Of domestic animals, zebu, the humped cattle of the island, are by far the most important. They are well adapted to the arid lands of the south, where the Bara, Antandroy, and Mahafaly keep large herds and lead a pastoral life. Every morning at dawn the men take the cattle to graze in the grasslands, returning with them at dusk. The sight of large herds stretching out across the open landscape in the rich light of early morning and late afternoon is stirring indeed.

In the dry season the use of the pasture lands has to be very carefully monitored. The herd must be split up to assess which beasts can be safely taken to the most distant grazing land and which are too weak for the long trek. The continuity of the clan herds is expressed in the marks cut into the ears of the cattle. They are called *sofindrazana*, the ancestral ear.

Like pastoralists in East Africa, those of southern Madagascar do not live off cattle products. As much as possible they survive on what crops they can grow, including rice. Cattle are used in dowries and are sold to raise money to pay for other goods, but they are rarely if ever slaughtered for their meat. They are, however, used in sacrifices throughout the island. Even in the forests, where cattle are not herded at all, they are brought in when major ceremonies take place. For lesser events chickens may sometimes be used. Only the Vezo on the coast systematically use other creatures in sacrifice.

It might seem that few cattle end up being slaughtered if they are mainly killed in sacrifice. Yet, the number of such ceremonies is surprising. In the days preceding the famadihana, Rakotoarivo supervised seven sacrifices. Always, before slaughter, an invocation to the ancestors was spoken. Each sacrifice was in honor of the razana and in the expectation of the benefits that flow from them.

Other occasions come to mind. The maiden flight of the jumbo jet operated by Air Madagascar was preceded by the sacrifice of zebu. I was also once invited to a housewarming party by a prominent doctor; again a zebu was slaughtered. The invocation at the sacrifice sought to place the new residence under ancestral protection. The skull still sits on the balcony.

If by these acts Air Madagascar flies with ancestral blessing, or a fashionable home rests under the protection of the razana, would it not be wise for environmental policy to include respect for the ways of the ancestors?

The "valiha," a stringed bamboo zither popular in the highlands, is a musical instrument of Southeast Asian origin, one of many examples of Malayo/ Polynesian influences in Malagasy culture. Painting by Rainimaharosoa.

Outrigger canoes plying the Mozambique Channel echo the first settlement of Madagascar, the last great landmass save for Antarctica to be colonized by humans, less than 2,000 years ago. Seafarers, believed to have originated from Indonesia, arrived via India and Africa, adopting new customs along the way.

An Antankarana woman sells bottled condiments on the spice island of Nosy Be, where the scent of vanilla and ylang-ylang fills the air (left). An Antambahoaka king poses with the regalia of his honored position in the east coast village of Ambohitsara, where a 14th-century stone elephant from India sits unexplained. A Betsileo girl from a village near Fianarantsoa wears the finely braided hair and brimless raffia hat that typify her people. These faces reflect influences of Asia, Africa, and Arabia in the remarkable amalgam of Malagasy culture.

The Malagasy language is rich with proverbs and poetic images spoken by a people in love with oratory. Any occasion, such as this wake for which people have gathered on a chilly morning near Ambalavao (left), calls for speeches, or "kabary," punctuated with references to the old ways. The great majority of Malagasy still live in small villages such as Ambatofirahana (right), where

farmers tilling the land put more faith in ways that served their ancestors than in benefits that modern technology might yield.

Taboos, or "fady," govern all aspects of public and private life, from the correct way to approach a house to the best sleeping position.

In Madagascar a person upon death is sometimes given a new name before entering the ranks of the ancestors, the "razana," who govern the living from their vantage point in eternity. Ancestors appear in dreams and apparitions and permeate the course of everyday life on all levels of society. The most flamboyant manifestation of the Malagasy connection with the hereafter is the practice of "famadihana," or turning of the dead. In the highlands where Merina and Betsileo people enshrine their dead in family graves, many tombs are opened every year during the cold winter months. Amid festivities, including music, dancing, sit-down meals, and, of course, speeches, the remains of ancestors are taken out and wrapped in new shrouds of the finest material available. At right, a famadihana party near Avaratriniala carries newly wrapped remains and old family portraits back to the tomb. Below, a fresh corpse is consigned to a tomb near Ambatolampy, decorated with traditional designs and topped by Christian crosses.

Giddy from the effect of toka gasy, *a potent local rum, Antandroy women dance their way home from a funeral near Amboasary.*

OVERLEAF

Cattle blood colors a sacred "hazó manga" pole cut from a "katrafay" tree and erected east of a newly elected clan chief's hut. The blood signifies fertility and clan solidarity during an elaborate ceremony in a Mahafaly village near Betioky, known as a stronghold of traditions.

A Tanala woman carrying a goose to the market; an Antandroy woman balancing an old iron heated by charcoal; a Mahafaly woman transporting a cherished sewing machine. On average these and other Malagasy women can expect to live 51 years and bear 6 children. The status of women in Madagascar varies by region and class. Hemmed in by taboos and traditions, they rarely attain positions of authority in village affairs but may wield great influence behind the scenes and in family matters. Only in the more privileged strata of society is it common to see women in powerful public roles.

OVERLEAF

Paddies on the outskirts of Antananarivo gleam green with rice. After setbacks in the 1970s, Madagascar is again reaching for self-sufficiency in rice production as prices rise in a free market.

A Betsileo girl carries rice shoots from a nursery to a paddy near Fianarantsoa, where they are planted by hand. Rice is the preferred staple food for most Malagasy; without it no meal is complete. Their per capita consumption of a pound per day is the world's second highest, exceeded only by Burmese people. Rice, or "vary," permeates Malagasy thinking. Scores of proverbs refer to rice, and the number of ways it can be described in the Malagasy language rivals the Inuit vocabulary for snow.

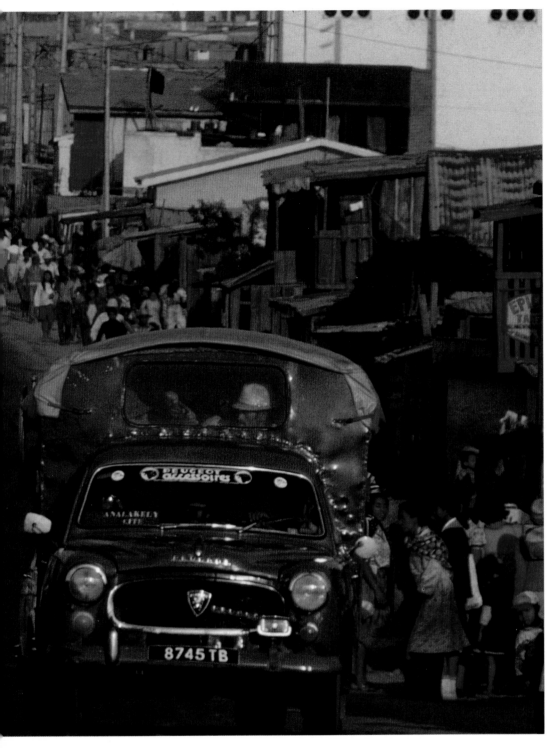

Sad indicator of economic depression, homeless children have become an increasing presence on the streets of Antananarivo, a city of a million people that shows the strain of the economic malaise of the past two decades. During that period per capita annual income slipped to $210. The majority of the island's households do not earn enough to feed themselves, and malnutrition is widespread.

Guardians of the maritime skills that aided the first immigrants to the island, the Vezo, the "people-of-the-paddle," are the only Malagasy who maintain an orientation toward the sea. Their lightweight pirogues, delicately crafted from select wood obtained in the dry forest, are the only indigenous sailing craft on the west coast.

"Dark-the-mouth-of-the-cooking-pot" ("maizim-bana-vilamy") is the Malagasy term for the hour of twilight, a time when Vezo girls, carrying copper water vessels reminiscent of India, gather around the underground well that gave their village its name, Andavadoaka, meaning "hole-in-the-rock" (left).

To eight-year-old Voitsikiavao, the cry of curlews signals the monthly low tide, when shorebirds and Vezo people all probe the tidal lagoons for octopus and shellfish (above).

To Mazista, a 65-year-old man whose face has been weathered by a life at sea, age brings respect but no reprieve from hardship. As an elder, or "hazo manga," his voice is heard in his community, but as head of a family of five living in a hut on the beach, he still has to spend long nights at sea to feed his children. Even in his remote village, where most people live on the fringe of a cash economy, hard economic realities are felt at the village store. The prices of bare necessities such as cooking oil and cotton cloth have gone up, while the price of fish has gone down. For Mazista it means that a simple spool of nylon needed to replace a fishing net is now beyond his reach.

More than any other Malagasy, Vezo people maintain an immediate connection with wildlife. Fish to these hunters and gatherers is as important as rice is to people elsewhere. Instead of chickens, they keep egrets taken young from mangrove rookeries. Birds are symbols of fertility in their cosmology: Vezo tombs, hidden in the bush, are crowned by erotic sculptures that include scenes of intercourse between men and birds. And while other Malagasy revere cattle, some Vezo treat sea turtles with a ritual accord evoking parallels with human burial rites elsewhere on the island. The head of a hawksbill turtle, or ''hara'' (Eretmochelys imibricata), has been impaled on a stake in a village near Morombe. The hunter who brought the turtle ashore decorated the bow of his canoe with its blood and shared the meat with village elders at a designated turtle cemetery, where the shell is piled on top of others harvested previously. The head will be left to decay on a stake until it drops to the ground. Only then is the turtle considered truly dead and its spirit released, whereupon the head can be tossed back into the sea the next time a turtle is brought ashore. Few Vezo practice this ritual to its full extent today. The tides of change, exacerbated by economic pressure, are diluting older ways. It has been reported that a dolphin washing up dead on a beach would once have been treated by Vezo like one of their own kin. Wrapped in shrouds, it would be buried next to humans in a cemetery. Today it is more common to hear stories of dolphins, or ''fesoke,'' harpooned for food.

ON THE EDGE OF SURVIVAL

Alison Jolly

*Tsy misy ala, tsy misy rano,
tsy misy vary.*

Without the forest, there will
be no more water,
without water, there will be
no more rice.

MALAGASY SAYING

*After centuries of environmental
abuse, much of Madagascar's
interior lies barren. Although the
extent of original forest cover is still
debated, it is undisputed that its
demise has accelerated erosion by
rains that create deep gullies, or
"lavaka." The combined impact of
rain leaching minerals away and
sun baking unshaded earth is a
sterile soil called laterite, where only
coarse bunch grass thrives, of little
use to man or beast.*

Here is a paradox. Madagascar is one of the world's poorest countries. It is also one of those most ravaged by erosion. Forests that once blanketed the land now cover perhaps 15 percent, and they shrink while you watch. Yet a conservationist friend said to me, "With all the money and goodwill it has going for it, Madagascar should make it if any place can."

I am not sure my friend is right. I think Madagascar's future is now in the balance. A millennium and a half of tradition says that nature is there to be exploited, that more children mean more wealth, and that economic pressures pass down the line from rich to poor, who then use up the capital of forest and soil. Only a decade of increased environmental awareness now confronts those traditions.

It was in 1979 that the World Wildlife Fund first became active in Madagascar. Five years later every government minister signed a policy document called the Strategy for Conservation and Sustainable Development. In 1985, Madagascar made that strategy public by holding an International Conference on the Environment for aid donors, scientists, and Malagasy administrators.

In 1989 Barber Conable, president of the World Bank, came to visit Madagascar at the invitation of the Malagasy government. Conable met with government ministers not only in the capital city but at a small hotel in the eastern rain forest. There he heard the outline for a 15-year Environmental Action Plan to set Madagascar on a course of sustainable development. He walked in the forest, he watched a Parson's chameleon snap up grasshoppers with a tongue longer than its own body, and he heard indri sing. He saw charred hillsides, cleared for slash-and-burn fields, and spoke about methods the rain forest farmers might try in order to live sustainably within their own region. Then he helicoptered off for discussions the same day with President Ratsiraka of Madagascar and President Arap Moi of Kenya.

Environmental awareness has become an international priority. There can hardly be a president, a politician, or a head of a United Nations agency who does not know that nature is now too small and too fragile to survive if our species continues to use up resources unthinkingly.

How did that change in awareness come about in Madagascar, and what does it mean for the future?

SLOW FRONTIER: THE EASTERN RAIN FOREST

Madagascar was one of the last habitable land masses to be settled by human beings. Our species arrived only about 1,500 years ago. Those first people found a land of forests and tree savannas, elephant birds and giant lemurs. The people spread through the land. They brought various traditions from Africa, Indonesia, and the Persian Gulf. Above all, they learned to adapt their traditions to the ecology of the regions where they lived.

The Malagasy were, and are, a frontier people. They did not just adapt to the land, they changed it. There are few Malagasy who are at home in the

forest the way Amazonian Indians are. The only candidates are the Mikea, part-time hunter-gatherers. It is not clear whether they preserve old traditions or whether they are dispossessed villagers forced into marginal outlaw lives— no more aboriginal than Robin Hood.

Most Malagasy are like 19th-century Americans, who cleared as they went. Madagascar was a slow frontier; people had time to recycle slash-and-burn (or *tavy*) clearings. The assumption was that there would always be enough land on the frontier. The Malagasy have a proverb for boundless love or friendship:

There will be no end like the eastern forest.
Rahanoriana no lany ny ala atsinana

In the eastern rain forest itself and on the flat lands of the east coast, the tradition is paddy rice in the valleys and tavy on the slopes. Dr. Jean Louis Rakotomanana, a member of the National Institute for Agricultural Research, describes tavy clearings among the people of Beforona in the central Betsileo region (Beforona means "the place where many assemble"). There are "free" lands where anyone may make a field, though you are expected to observe a seven-year fallow. There are also clan lands, centered round the family tomb, with a mandatory ten-year fallow, and permission of the clan leader is needed before cutting. The trouble is that more and more forest is cut on a four- or five-year cycle, which the villagers themselves know to be too short. A cleared tavy field of mountain rice or manioc on a 40 degree slope (about three–quarters of the land has a greater slope) loses about 500 metric tons of topsoil per year. Population growth and the loss of soil fertility mean people must cut higher and higher into the forest, until only the topmost ridges hold trees, like a mohawk haircut above bald slopes below. No wonder villagers are closely watching Dr. Rakotomanana's experiments in agroforestry. Planting fast-growing trees on contour lines may hold the soil on those bare hillsides and let them become permanent fields.

The rain forest has not only been cut for subsistence farming: Most of Madagascar's export crops are grown on the eastern coast. Though there are some large plantations of sugar, oranges, and bananas, the most significant exports—coffee, vanilla, and clove—are grown by small farmers who sell to marketing cartels. Each small plantation is a little pockmark in the forest. The world price of coffee has dropped threefold in the past five years. Clove has dropped even more. Madagascar sells 90 percent of the world's vanilla, but this is threatened by biotechnology. If laboratories in the U.S. succeed in coming up with a synthetic substitute for true vanilla essence, some 70,000 Malagasy families will lose their livelihood overnight. This is not to imply that Malagasy should give up on agricultural exports. It does show that neither families nor the nation can foresee survival without subsistence agriculture. The 1987 per capita income was $210—that is, if an average Malagasy offered all she produced in both cash and subsistence goods, the world would pay her $210 for the year's production.

It is clear from fossils, and fossil pollen, that in historic times the eastern forest stretched from the sea to far onto the plateau. Cores taken of lake sediments show that if you go still further back, there were periods when the

Well into the 19th century, houses in the highlands were made of wood, including those in Antananarivo seen here surrounding the Queen's Palace. Deforestation of the highlands necessitated new building techniques, and today most houses are built from mud bricks.

eastern forest was even more fragmented than it is today. Eighteen thousand years ago at the height of the last glacial period the rain forest at Andasibe, where the World Bank president watched indri, was montane heath like the highest Malagasy mountains today. The rain forest ecosystems have moved uphill and down, spreading and retracting inch by inch on a time scale of millennia. They have never faced a threat like today's, when they could be scraped wholly bare in the next 20 years.

THE SPINY DESERT

People of the north and west also make tavy fields. They clear the forest to plant corn. These lands are flatter than the slopes of the eastern rain forest escarpment, but they regenerate forest cover slowly for lack of rain.

Botanists of the Swiss Sustainable Forestry Project at Morondava have tried to work out a sustainable logging cycle for such forests. Near Morondava there may be no rain at all for nine months of the year. During the three-month wet season downpours alternate with unpredictable ten-day dry spells. In these woodlands most plants are deciduous, with neither leaves nor new growth during winter's drought. Even in the wet season, seedlings of some species may grow only once in five years or more. It takes one good uninterrupted wet season to germinate viable seed, and another one the next year for a seedling to grow enough to survive. A tree whose life span is measured in centuries can afford a five- or ten-year birth interval. A tavy farmer cannot afford a century-long cutting cycle. It looks increasingly as though sustainable logging requires much larger areas and longer cutting intervals than the Swiss originally predicted.

People and most animals cannot live in such a place without water. Thankfully, sedimentary rocks of the west hold small permanent ponds as well as streams that carry underground water even though the surface sand is dry. Such places abound with life—birds bathe, red-fronted lemurs drink, sifaka browse on succulent foliage. These rich nerve centers of the forest are also the first to be cleared to make room for a village and a few fields.

DRY FOREST OF THE WEST

The spiny desert looks as though it could defend itself. The vicious geometry of thorns and an invisible armory of plant poisons defend it against cattle, although goats can eat young plants even here. Paradoxically the forest is too dry to burn. There is not enough leaf litter to carry flames, and the water-storing trunks will not catch fire. Grass fires that sweep the savannas stop at the forest edge. The soil is far too dry for normal crops, so there is no point in making tavy fields. It would seem as though the spiny desert forest might stand forever. Instead it may be one of the first natural formations to disappear completely. It is being cut down, tree by tree, for timber and for charcoal. The roads to Tulear and to Tolagnaro are lined with the huts of charcoal burners, and the forest is rolled back. The tall *Didiereaceae*, which look so much like candelabra cactuses, have a woody interior unlike a cactus's spongy flesh. They provide the planks for houses. Other trees, scarcely more than gnarled thorn bushes, are turned into fuel.

ILLUSTRATION BY ARTHUR SZYK FROM THE HERITAGE PRESS BOOK *THE ARABIAN NIGHTS ENTERTAINMENTS*, VOLUME I.

During one of the seven voyages recounted in A Thousand and One Nights, *Sindbad the Sailor, the legendary 13th-century explorer, describes how he is airlifted by a giant bird called Roc, which was perhaps inspired by stories of Madagascar's elephant bird, then still extant.*

In Madagascar most art of consequence is connected to funerary rites, and no architecture is more important than the construction of tombs. According to one study, a sizable portion of the gross national product is spent on funerary activities. Unproductive though this may seem to Westerners, it makes perfect sense to Malagasy, who reason: "One is willing to spend most on the house in which one is to dwell the longest."

One compounding factor is that the spiny desert is so varied. Stands of Didiereaceae grow only in localized spots. One of the best patches lines the road between Tolagnaro and Amboasary Sud. Passing tourists admire it and take pictures of the charcoal burners. Tourists imagine the same lunar landscapes stretch beyond the road, that they are only seeing the fringes of the forest. In fact, they are cutting through the center. Beyond the landscape they survey, there is not much more.

Gallery forest in the south presents a similar problem of patches. Beside the few great rivers, spreading tamarind trees can grow on alluvial soil. These forests are rich natural habitat for ring-tailed lemurs, flying foxes, and birds of prey. Preliminary investigation by Robert Sussman and Glen Green of Washington University suggest that only about a thousand hectares of closed-canopy gallery forest now remain intact. Much of that lies in the tiny reserves of Beza-Mahafaly and Berenty. Since many scientists and tourists—and seemingly all television teams—go to Berenty, we often picture "typical" Madagascar as a great green tamarind tree full of ring-tailed lemurs. In fact, such forests were probably always rare, and they were among the first places where people installed their fields.

FIRE ON THE SAVANNAS

About 85 percent of Madagascar is not forest but fields and savannas. There has been a continuing controversy over whether the savannas have always existed or whether they were made by man and his fires.

In the 1920s it was argued that the savannas were man-made, based on the paucity of endemic species. Madagascar's forests boast 80-percent species endemicity in the rain forest, and 95 percent in the spiny desert. On the savannas, by contrast, grow common African and Javan grasses. If the savanna has existed as long as the forest, then Madagascar should have evolved an endemic grassland flora as well.

Recently, David Burney of Fordham University has drilled pollen cores that give a different picture. He suggests there was tree savanna on the plateau hills, with acacias and other trees dotting parklike grasslands. In little cups where there are now paddy fields grew clumps of rich evergreen forest, home to giant lemurs and to plants now confined to rain forest.

Robert Dewar of the University of Connecticut has suggested that before people arrived, the savannas were grazed by giant tortoises, pygmy hippos, elephant birds, and *Hadrophithcus*, a ground-dwelling lemur. These creatures had a different choice of plants than African ungulates and were probably less efficient grazers than ungulates. When people came, they brought with them that magnificent African ungulate, the humped long-horned zebu. Grazing zebu then eliminated the local plants, leaving only tougher forms that had evolved with the hoofed mammals of the African plains.

Thus, though humans probably did not originate the savanna, people, zebu, and fire maintain the savanna in its present-day form.

It has been estimated that one-fourth to one-third of Madagascar burns every year. People set fires to burn the grasslands. There is a saying—"well finished, or well prepared, like the burned lands."

Why does burning seem good to the Malagasy? First, burned grass regrows rapidly, providing pasturage for zebu at the end of the dry season. The carrying capacity for cattle is not determined by the total annual productivity of the land, but by the animals' ability to survive the worst season. In the long term, however, burning leads to tougher, less palatable grasses that keep nutrients in their roots, where neither fire nor grazing cattle can reach them. Foreign advisors suggest making hay from the palatable grasses; Malagasy prefer to burn to survive the seasonal crisis. Their lives are stretched thin enough without inventing new, apparently unnecessary tasks.

A second reason for burning the hills is to increase water runoff to the rice paddies below. Again foreigners are horrified: Increased runoff leads to increased erosion. If the rice can be planted sooner, however, it has a longer growing season or can be brought to market more quickly. Again the peasants' reasoning is based on a clear short-term gain.

A final factor is political protest. As politicians are elected, they begin to see the long-term implications. Fire degrades the soil and the yield. The government sends out posters and stamps and campaigns by radio with the message: "Burning the hillsides is burning the nation!" In election years, and years of great hardship, peasants can send back the message that they would like to burn the nation—literally.

PADDY RICE OF THE PLATEAU

Indonesian sailors came to Madagascar bringing the seeds and the technology of paddy rice. A well-known Malagasy tale, the Legend of Self-Created, tells of the triumph of rice over hillside crops like manioc. Self-Created was a farmer who burned the hillsides to grow root crops. The smoke of burning forests irritated God's eyes in heaven. Self-Created kept his fire alight in spite of God's curses and thunderstorms. In the end, by sheer audacity, Self-Created won the hand of God's daughter, the Sky Princess. Together they smuggled rice, the food of the gods, back to earth.

Everywhere in Madagascar rice is the preferred, aristocratic food: a great heaped pile of rice that fills the plate, with a little well for stew or sauce dimpling the top. In the many valleys and the few large plains of the plateau, society revolves around rice fields.

Paddy rice requires care and labor: trampling the field, planting the nursery field, transplanting, weeding, water control, harvest. The infrastructure of dikes and irrigation ditches needs constant attention. Plateau marriages were traditionally between cousins or adjacent landholders to keep the precious rice lands within the family.

Land tenure is now one of the chief environmental problems for the people of the plateau. Many properties belong to absentee landlords, while tenants sharecrop. Landlords prefer to lease for only one growing season—a tenant

Tombs found among the Mahafaly and Antandroy in the south rank among the most elaborate funerary architecture found in the African region today. Some of the largest "tombeaus" take dozens of artisans more than a year to complete and may measure 30 by 30 meters. Decorations include paintings illustrating popular stories (above). Airplanes top some tombs: Originally referring to a trip once taken by the deceased lying below, airplanes have become common designs now, perhaps conferring prestige. Tomb architecture keeps evolving, an indication of the strength of an indigenous art form rooted in tradition.

One of only a handful of trained Malagasy botanists, Armand Rakotozafy of Parc Tsimbazaza examines a pachypodium tree in Bemaraha reserve.

with long tenure might claim rights to the land. Such leaseholders have no interest in planting trees or checking long-term erosion. This in turn increases the pressure for fuelwood from native forests.

Some villages, however, have rights to their land. Among them, Swiss foresters, religious development organizations, and one Malagasy agroforestry enterprise are promoting integrated tree-cropping as well as the use of compost fertilizer. Peasants increasingly attempt to plant fruit trees and fuelwood trees, to experiment with dry-land off-season crops on the hillsides, and to cut hillside grass for compost instead of burning it up.

These people have long accepted the constraints and hard work of settled agriculture. If they can find low-risk ways to improve their land, they will do so. An idealist might even dream of Madagascar leapfrogging past the stage of chemical fertilizers and pesticides to export "organic" strawberries, cherries, and lychees that would shock the West by having real taste.

For now, however, farmers must cope with *lavaka*, the scourge of the paddy fields. Lavaka are erosion gullies that pour red laterite landslides into those painfully constructed fields. Laterite is subject to sheet erosion, like any other soil, but the exposed crust can bake brick-hard in the sun. The soft lower layers then undercut at the gully's head, in a process more like earth-moving than erosion. This is a lavaka. The gullies can be stabilized—there are many old lavaka where vegetation grows back. Active lavaka, though, are relentless. They bisect ridge roads, suffocate fields, and even swallow buildings. In a World Bank–funded irrigation scheme at Lac Alaotra—the rice bowl of Madagascar—fields now silt up as fast as they can be created.

THE CITIES

At first glance Madagascar's urban environment is beautiful. The 19th-century gables of Antananarivo cling to the slopes like a rosy Italian hill town. Tolagnaro and Antseranana overlook cobalt blue bays sheltered from the Indian Ocean. French-built arcades and rows of royal palms give stately hearts to Toamasina and Hellville, and even their shantytowns have traditional layered coconut thatch, with orchids and begonias blooming in old tin cans on the tiny porches.

The second impression, though, is that the cities are dirty. Even Antananarivo has running water and sewage for only a small minority of its inhabitants. Garbage collection is mainly the job of scavengers: dogs, crows, and people. (Admittedly in this poor country, very little is thrown away. It is only recently that hotels here understood that tourists throw something away every day and expect a wastebasket in every room.) Attempts to manage the problem of human waste have met with little success. Noisome public toilets lead to drains that too often lead to open canals, and the canal bank becomes the more acceptable place for relief.

Industrial pollution will arrive soon if it hasn't already. Polluted air belches from antique trucks and buses. (The average vehicle in Madagascar is 15 years old.) Public transport is a perpetual problem, though somewhat eased recently by a gift of buses from Japan.

All these problems will increase. Madagascar is still 80 percent rural, but urban migration is underway. The one advantage Madagascar has is that it can confront the future while its towns are still fairly small: Most have a population of less than 100,000; only Antananarivo holds more than a million.

POPULATION

Madagascar's total population was about 11.25 million in 1989, growing at 3.1 percent per year. That means that by 2015 the population if unchecked will triple, or if strong family-planning programs succeed, will merely double.

Surprisingly, Madagascar could probably support double or even triple its present population. More intensive farming, more land under cultivation, could maintain a nation of subsistence farms, but if it gained a source of exports, it could do far better. Japan has ten times Madagascar's population on two-thirds of its land area, with 75 times its per capita income.

Today, for most Malagasy, children represent wealth. They represent wealth in terms of pride and love and social security. They also represent hard cash: A child can help in the field at age six and herd cattle at eight. Westerners and Malagasy elite agonize over the cost of a child—so many thousands of dollars just to have it born in hospital, let alone send it to college—but a rural Malagasy child pays its keep and more. Westerners view parents of large families as irresponsibly squandering their family means. Malagasy view this Western attitude as an attack on the well-being only a large family can bring, as well as on love and pride.

There is, to be sure, a large unmet need for family planning—to space children, to guard older mothers' health, or, in rare cases, to let a young girl finish her studies. There are now proposals before the legislature to institute government family-planning programs.

Other needs—education, infant health care, a higher standard of living—must also be met if population growth is to be slowed. Elite Malagasy and the government itself are now well aware that change must come. This is an island, and it could sooner or later become simply too full. The way to voluntary change, however, is for families to grow richer and more secure. Increased poverty leads to increased population, until real famine provides the Malthusian guillotine.

THE GREENHOUSE EFFECT

The greenhouse effect is the change in the earth's climate as a result of carbon dioxide and other gases emitted by industry, by burning fossil fuel, and by burning forest. It could be potentially devastating to Madagascar. All predictions are currently uncertain. The general consensus is that we might expect about two degrees centigrade of global warming in the next thirty years. Those who agree with the consensus are unwilling to declare what that means for any one area. Even so, it is very clear that if temperature and rainfall patterns change, the wild plants and animals, already limited to small reserves, will have no way to escape to more favorable habitats.

The humble rosy periwinkle, or "trongatse" (Catharanthus roseus), a weed that grows commonly around villages, has become a celebrated example of the potential use of Malagasy medicinal plants. Western scientists analyzing claims of trongatse's healing potential discovered powerful alkaloids in the plant that became the basis of a miracle drug that now stems childhood leukemia. One hundred tons of dried periwinkle roots are exported from Madagascar each year, and the plant has inspired a multimillion-dollar industry. Sadly, the financial benefits accrue mostly to Western pharmaceutical firms. Little is known about the other five kinds of periwinkle native to Madagascar except that they are becoming rare.

Simultaneously, if long-cultivated crops are no longer suited to the areas where people are used to growing them, there will be massive disruption in agricultural nations like Madagascar.

Madagascar contributes yearly to the greenhouse effect by its burning of forests, its burning of grasslands, and by the methane that oozes from its rice paddies. It has the potential, however, to be one of the places that helps the world to stabilize its climate. If there were an international fund to plant and safeguard trees, in the millions of square kilometers the world needs, Madagascar could be a major beneficiary. The lands of Madagascar's "midwest" now stand bare. They are too sterile for most agriculture, too raked by fire for anything but the thinnest pasture. They are no source of biodiversity— the native plants of the region died out long ago. If an overheating world could pay Madagascar to plant hardy fast-growing trees, there is land enough to become a major "carbon sink." Of course the payments would have to trickle down to peasant level to ensure that farmers protected the new plantations rather than setting them on fire.

A DECADE OF CHANGE

In the 19th century, under Merina rule, the felling of virgin forest was forbidden. On the coast there were traditional cutting cycles that prescribed minimum times for forest fallow.

French and English scientists pointed out Madagascar's uniqueness to the rest of the world. In 1927 the French colonial government created the first nature reserves in the African region. These were a series of "Reserves Integrales," chosen for their scientific (botanical) value, and for their remoteness from human invasion. No one was supposed to enter without a research permit. In practice that meant foreign scientists only. There were also two national parks, the Isalo massif and the Montagne d'Ambre, open to the public but in actuality only accessible to people with cars.

The educational system before 1975 was wholly French, complete with a children's history book that began "Our ancestors, the Gauls. . . ." Primary school science dealt with wine making and rabbits in the snow. A student who reached high school and who studied biology eventually learned there were unique species in the French dependency of Madagascar. Meanwhile, city-dwelling Malagasy considered life at the forest edge to be backward and primitive.

In the countryside, the people who lived from the land commonly regarded city folk and government officers as enemies. Foresters were a quasi-military force who forbade traditional slash-and-burn cultivation on steep slopes or in valuable timber stands. Agricultural extension workers preached against pasture burning but often had no immediately useful techniques to offer. Conservation of soil, forest, or wildlife seemed like a burden, not a benefit.

In 1970 Madagascar held its first International Conference on the Preservation of Nature. This conference brought together Malagasy officials and distinguished foreign conservationists like Charles Lindbergh and Peter Scott, founder of the World Wildlife Fund. In an atmosphere of hope, exhortations and promises were made, but nothing really happened. The "revolution" of 1972–1975 was a largely peaceful change to socialist government, but the foreign links dissolved. From 1975 to 1984 official policy was that the environment could be ignored. There was too much else to do. In the late 1970s a policy of "all-out investment" staked Madagascar's future to rapid industrialization. Then, in the 1980s, it became clear that most of the investments had failed. Crippling national debt was all that remained. The International Monetary Fund dictated a policy of structural adjustment—belt-tightening—to put the economy in order. That left almost nothing for "luxuries": health services, education, agricultural extension work, or the infrastructure of environmental protection.

In spite of the economic crisis, a few Malagasy kept a longer vision of the relation of people to their land. Dr. Barthelemi Vaohita, Madagascar's representative of the World Wildlife Fund, persisted in his drive for education at all levels, from schoolchild to the country's ministers. Dr. Gilbert Ravelojaona, president of the Madagascar University School of Agriculture, set up a wildlife reserve at Beza-Mahafaly in the southwest, collaborating with Yale University and Washington University in St. Louis. At times such initiatives seemed as though they might drown in opposition or indifference, but by 1984 these voices could again be heard.

In 1984 the government ministers signed a "National Strategy for Conservation and Sustainable Development." In October 1985 they made their new policy spectacularly public. They held a second International Conference, inviting foreign-aid donors, foreign scientists, and several hundred Malagasy from around the country. Joseph Randrianasolo, then Minister of Livestock, Water, and Forests, explained the change in attitudes: "Before," he declared, "people only spoke of the beauty and scientific interest of our flora and fauna.

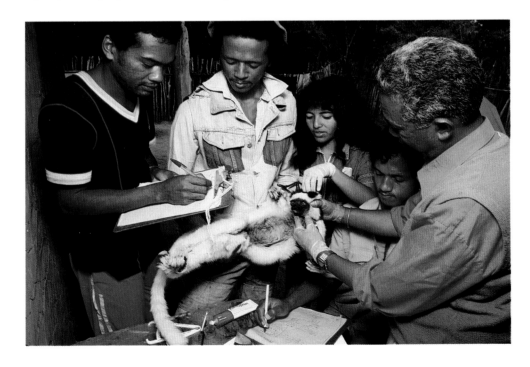

Potain Rakotomanga and students from the University of Madagascar examine an anesthetized sifaka before releasing it back into its troop in the new reserve of Beza-Mahafaly. Villagers donated their sacred forest as part of an innovative effort combining plans for conservation with local development needs.

This time we are speaking of our people and how to manage our resources to be self-sufficient in food and fuelwood." Remy Tiandrazana of the Revolutionary Council put it more bluntly: "We have before us the specter of Ethiopia."

In the course of the conference, Minister Randrianasolo opened the Beza Reserve—the first new wild land preserve established since the 1950s. Beza is not just a place for fundamental research but an experiment in integrated development. The neighboring Mahafaly villagers dedicated their sacred forest for science and gave up their own rights to pasture their herds in the woods. In return they will receive agronomic advice, a road to take their crops to market, and a canal for irrigation. And the scientists will learn from the villagers about medicinal plants. The channels of communication stay open between villagers, Malagasy professors and students from the capital, and foreign visitors.

Beza has become a model for increasing support to many forests in Madagascar's "necklace of pearls." The limestone pinnacles of the tsingy of Bemaraha will become a UNESCO World Heritage site. The aye ayes' home at Mananara is already a UNESCO Biosphere Reserve. The World Wildlife Fund has set as one priority the complex of habitats in the far north—rain forest on the ancient volcano of the Montagne d'Ambre, nearby dry forest harboring a tiny population of black sifaka, and the crocodile caves of the Ankarana. Farther south, the WWF focuses on Marojejy, a precipitous rain forest massif, as well as on the mountain range of Andringitra, whose heath-clad summits separate the eastern rain forest from the western plateau. U.S. AID supports not only Beza but also the huge reserve of Andohahaela, straddling the "rainfall fault-line" of the extreme southeast, where mountain rain forest grows next to the spiny desert. U.S. AID and the Missouri Botanical Garden will help the newly declared National Park of the Masoala, Madagascar's only remaining lowland rain forest and the home of the forest coconut and red-ruffed lemur. Finally, Ranomafana's rain forest has also been declared a national park. Duke University is spearheading the conservation of Ranomafana's golden bamboo lemur and the renaissance of the entire region.

All these efforts concentrate on particular areas, using the energy of the few available trained people to push the reserves and their regions toward mutual progress. This is the sort of action that will achieve results, though much more is needed to reach the other forests not yet adopted by a funding organization. What about more general concerns—the human and economic environment of the country?

To set Madagascar on a national path of sustainable development, an improbable alliance has been forged among the government, the World Bank, the World Wildlife Fund (now called in Europe the World-Wide Fund for Nature), Conservation International, and other nonprofit groups. In November of 1989, the WWF celebrated its tenth year in Madagascar by opening an environmental teaching center in Tsimbazaza Zoo (the only zoo and the only such center in the country). During that decade, while promoting the change in official attitude, WWF has surveyed the forests of Madagascar, produced a handbook of all reserves and conservation priorities, and participated in reserve administration. It has initiated a program of elementary school environment education. Its Environmental Action Plan has now been transformed into a major initiative of the World Bank.

The Bank is perhaps the largest single economic influence in Madagascar, assuming much of the intimate role in the nation's affairs that the French ceded in 1975. The country depends on Bank-funded projects, such as the overhaul of primary education. Madagascar is too poor and too much in debt to do otherwise.

The government's conversion to environmentalism, with the 1985 conference, came at just the right time: The Bank was looking for a project that would demonstrate its own environmental awareness. Madagascar filled the bill.

The National Environmental Action Plan—now a multidonor, multiministry program—includes sections on biodiversity, on land surveying and land tenure, on soil conservation and agroforestry, on training for the people needed to carry out these programs, and on education for all. After two years of negotiation involving at least 150 Malagasy experts and scores of participants from the Bank and other donors, Madagascar has established a National Fund for the Environment and a National Bureau for the Environment to administer the fund. It is still in the process of reaching the people. Perhaps in the next few years we will begin to see results at the level that counts—the farmer who must choose whether to plant a tree for fuel and harvest grass for compost, or to burn the land in the fashion of his ancestors.

The Environmental Action Plan is a 15-year project—three times as long as most of the Bank's plans, and longer than most elected politicians' vision in any country. It has taken just about a decade for Malagasy governmental opinion to change from outright denial that the environment could affect human welfare, to being one of the leading countries in at least the rhetoric of sound policy.

If the rhetoric does not become reality, there is no hope for Madagascar's fertile soil, its rivers, and its magic forests with their lemurs and tenrecs and vangas and couas and chameleons. But as Guy Razafindralambo of the Environmental Action Plan Support Group said to me, "We have no choice. We must succeed." Guy and I were driving between the blackened scars of 1989's tavy fields in the eastern rain forest. He waved a hand at the spreading landscape: the escarpment where stands of primeval rain forest perched on the ridge crests, second growth sprouted below, and charred new clearings were still smoking on either hand. In spite of the old proverb, the eastern forest was no longer endless.

"You can understand why we must succeed," he said. "If you desertify part of America there is always more. Even if the French destroyed France they could still walk to Germany or Switzerland. But if our environmental actions do not succeed, and we make a desert of Madagascar, what would we do? We'd have to swim!"

Reforestation schemes undertaken by the Malagasy government and supported by international aid stress the importance of new plantations of pine and eucalyptus as sources of firewood and construction materials. The trees also stabilize soil, as depicted in this drawing from a conservation brochure distributed to villagers.

Workers from a road-building project near the reserve of Analamazoatra survey the rapidly shrinking domain of the Malagasy rain forest.

A Betsimisaraka woman plants rice on a burnt hillside in the eastern rain forest while her husband cradles their children. Slash-and-burn agriculture, or "tavy," is a

Malagasy way of life rooted in long tradition, even though it yields only a fraction of the harvest accomplished in stable rice paddies. Traditionally, hillsides used for

growing rice would lie fallow for up to fifteen years, but economic pressures now force farmers to return to the same land in as little as five years, giving soil insufficient

chance to regenerate. To compensate for low yields, farmers clear new forest elsewhere, a leapfrogging vicious circle illegal by law but often tolerated by local officials, who realize that people have no easy alternatives. Forest areas once cleared become subject to annual fires set by villagers seeking to stimulate new grass growth, a "green bite," for their livestock. The end result: Every year much of the countryside goes up in smoke.

Antandroy, the proud "people-of-the-thorns," march through a parched sisal plantation during the drought that hit the south in 1985–86. Famine followed, claiming many lives and forcing thousands to leave their homes to try and eke out a living elsewhere. As Madagascar continues to lose its forests, the prospect of climate change, in particular the reduction of life-sustaining rainfall, is not unlikely. The specter of desertification—as befell the Sahel and already

shimmering in the sands and bleached bones near Cap St. Marie—looms in the distance.

A handful of skulls are all that is left of Madagascar's megafauna, which included lemurs bigger than humans. Clockwise from upper left, Megaladapis, Hadropithecus, Paleopropithecus, Archeolemur, and Archeoindris *witnessed the arrival of man on Madagascar but became extinct within centuries. The same tragic fate awaits a much larger array of unique Malagasy lifeforms unless action is taken today. Vositse, the giant jumping rat* (Hypogeomys antimena) *is in imminent danger of extinction. This strange nocturnal rodent, whose life history is practically unknown, has* the body of a rabbit, the tail of a rat, the nose of an elephant seal, and hops around like a little kangaroo in one restricted forest near Morondava that is rapidly being cleared. Crossley's babbler *(*Mystacornis crossleyi*), a shy song bird from the eastern rain forest, never before photographed, sits on a nest in the Analamazaotra reserve, within earshot of axes felling trees.*

The great majority of all Malagasy are subsistence farmers, cultivators of rice, maize, and manioc, for whom the notion of a hunting-gathering people on their own island is little more than a myth. Yet a small group of elusive forest people of mysterious origin do still exist. Leading hidden lives in the waterless forests of the west, bands of Mikea survive with skills reminiscent of Kalahari Bushmen. They dig for water-storing "babo" roots—their sole source of water for months—and search for "ovy ala," a wild sweet potato.

German biologist Bernhard Meier, here with Malagasy assistant Emile Rajery, shocked the scientific community in 1986 when he and Patricia Wright of Duke University discovered an unknown primate less than one kilometer off the road to Ranomafana. Before its existence became public knowledge, Lanting photographed the then anonymous creature munching bamboo. Now named the golden bamboo lemur (Hapalemur aureus), it is one of the world's most endangered primates. Only a few dozen individuals are known to survive.

Near Ranomafana, where the Namorona River drops over an escarpment and runs through a stretch of rain forest, recent scientific discoveries have prompted proposals for a new national park. Besides safeguarding a refuge for little-known creatures such as the Malagasy civet (Fossa fossana), the park would protect the watershed for villagers downstream.

At the edge of the Andasibe forest, frequented by tourists searching for lemurs, a young girl earns a few cents a day collecting medicinal herbs for a European pharmaceutical company. In a baobab forest near Analabe, destined to become a new nature reserve, a landless squatter displaced by drought in the south cuts trees to make room for a manioc plot to feed his family. These are the faces confronting conservationists trying to preserve Madagascar's natural treasures. To the poor, the forest is their last free meal, a resource to use today. Past conservation efforts failed because they were based on Western desires and did not accommodate local needs, but now hopeful new initiatives have been launched. Madagascar is becoming a test case for coalitions of international development and conservation organizations working in concert with government—which is rapidly waking up to the magnitude of its unique heritage.

OVERLEAF

Hubert Randrianasolo makes camp in a narrow canyon of the Ankarana reserve.

137

The evolutionary paths of mouse
lemur and man diverged many
millions of years ago when
Madagascar broke away from Africa,
but now, as our planet shrinks, we
are beginning to learn that our
destiny, or "vintana," may be
intertwined after all. In the image of
the whole earth, which has come to
symbolize the interconnectedness of
life, Madagascar is no longer an
island lost in time but an integral
part at the very center. The smallest
primate on earth and the most
powerful one share one ancestor in
the past and one world in the
future.

NASA APOLLO SATURN AS17

BIBLIOGRAPHY

Battistini, R., and Richard-Vindard, G. (eds), 1972. *Biogeography and ecology in Madagascar*. Mongraphiae biologicae 21, Junk, The Hague.

Bloch, M., 1971. *Placing the Dead, Tombs, Ancestral Villages and Kinship Organisation in Madagascar*. Seminar Press, London.

Bloch, M., and Parry, J. (eds), 1982. *Death and the Regeneration of Life*. Cambridge University Press, Cambridge.

Brown, M., 1978. *Madagascar Rediscovered*. Damien Tunnacliffe, London.

Catat, Louis, 1895. *Voyage á Madagascar 1889–1890*. Paris.

Flacourt, E. de, 1661. *Histoire de la Grande Isle de Madagascar*. Paris.

Fox, Leonard, 1990. *Hainteny: The Traditional Poetry of Madagascar*. Bucknell University Press, London.

Grandidier, A., 1908. *Ethnographie de Madagascar* (2 vols). Paris.

Jenkins, M.D. (ed), 1987. *Madagascar: An Environmental People*. IUCN, Cambridge.

Jolly, A., 1966. *Lemur Behavior*. University of Chicago Press, Chicago.

Jolly, A., Oberlé, P., and Albignac, R. *Key Environments: Madagascar*. Pergamon Press, Oxford.

Mack, J., 1986. *Madagascar: Island of the Ancestors*. British Museum Publication Limited, London.

Oberlé, P., 1981. *Madagascar, un sanctuaire de la nature*. Lechevalier S.A.R.L., Paris.

Petter, J-J, Albignac, R., and Runbler, Y., 1977. *Mammiféres Lemuriens (Primates Prosimiens)*. Faune de Madagascar 44, O.R.S.T.O.M., Paris.

Tattersall, I., 1982. *The Primates of Madagascar*. Columbia University Press, New York.

Tattersall, I., and Sussman, R.W., 1975. *Lemur Biology*. Plenum Press, New York.

ACKNOWLEDGMENTS

by Frans Lanting

I owe much to many.
Foremost among those who shaped my thinking about Madagascar is Alison Jolly. Others whose work and advice were important early on include Alison Richard and Robert Dewar. To John Mack I am thankful for sharing his insights into Malagasy culture.

I am indebted to many other researchers and experts who freely shared their knowledge and love of Madagascar: Roland Albignac, Jean Marie de la Beaujardière, Larry Dorr, Susan Dworski, Jörg Ganzhorn, Noel Gueunier, Lee Haring, Leonard Fox, Bernard Koechlin, Pete Lowry, Russell Mittermeier, Sheila O'Connor, Mark Pidgeon, Philippe Oberlé, Jean Jacques Petter, Fred Ramiandrasoa, M. Rabenoro, Martine Randriamanantenina, Jean Aimée Rakotorisoa, Armand Rakotozafy, S. Rakotofiringa, Peter Robinson, Elwyn Simons, Ian Tattersall, Neil Wells, and Patricia Wright are thanked hereby.

Work in Madagascar would have been much harder and less pleasant without the active support and logistical assistance of Kjetil Aano, M. Bang, Phil Chapman, Jean de Heaulme, Joseph Andrianjara, M. Jaosolo, Michael Griffin, M. Gérold, Rodrick Mast, H. Roger, Bernard Ramahafaly, Zinaha Razafindratandra, M. van Wijngaarden, Michel Rakotomirina, and many others.

I would especially like to thank the Malagasy government and in particular officials in the following departments for allowing and helping me to do field work in Madagascar: The Department of Water and Forestry, The Ministry of Higher Education, The Ministry of Scientific Research, The Directorate of Tourism, and Tsimbazaza Park.

Many organizations and institutions opened their doors and resources to me, including the Academie Malgache, Conservation International, Centre de Formation Professionelle Forestière, Duke Primate Center, Lutheran Mission, Missouri Botanical Garden, Norwegian Mission, Museum of Art and Archeology, University of Madagascar (Archeology and Zoology Departments) U.S. Embassy, World Wildlife Fund Madagascar, and World Wildlife Fund U.S.A. My sincerest thanks to them all.

In the private sector important support was provided by Air Madagascar, Amoco, Hotel Colbert, Madagascar Air Tours, Nikon Professional Services, Sobek, Société Rahariseta, and Fraise et Fils Cy.

My photographic work was commissioned by the National Geographic Society. Without its financial generosity and institutional support a project of this magnitude would not have been possible. I would like to express my gratitude especially to Bob Gilka, Rob Hernandez, Tom Kennedy, Kent Kobersteen, and last but not least to Bill Garrett.

I am indebted to Michael Hoffman at Aperture for taking the risk to publish this book. Bob Booth and Kay Kobor-Hankins helped with the production, but without the care and patience of Bob Madden, who oversaw the project from beginning to end, this book would not have been printed. Richard Minden's support throughout has been indispensable and is much appreciated.

To Christine Eckstrom my gratitude and love for her help and for being there sooner rather than later.

A handful of people in Madagascar deserve a special mention, for without their help and friendship my work could not have been accomplished. My gratitude goes to Olivier Langrand, Bernhard Meier, Martin Nicoll, André Peyrieras, Stan and Kathy Quanbeck and especially to Hubert Randrianasolo.

Native naturalists in Madagascar are as precious as the rarest flower. It was a privilege to work with two of the finest: Bedo Jaosolo and Georges Randrianasolo enriched the lives and knowledge of those who knew them. Their premature death is a great loss to Madagascar. Their love of nature has become part of this book.

Finally, I'd like to thank all of those who posed for me, drove me, sailed me, fed me, and sheltered me in villages around the island. At times my camp numbered up to a dozen companions and helpers for various tasks, evoking parallels with mountaineering expeditions, where the labor of many supports one man's reach for an unclimbed summit. But whereas the conquest of a mountaintop represents little but a personal triumph, I hope that this work, realized with the help of many, contributes to a greater understanding of a world in peril.

MISAOTRA BETSAKA

Library of Congress Catalog Number 90-081488

Paperback ISBN 0-89381-458-x
Hardcover ISBN 0-89381-422-9

The staff at Aperture for **Madagascar: A World Out of Time** is Michael E. Hoffman, Executive Director; Steve Dietz, Editor; Jane D. Marsching, Assistant Editor; Thomas Seelig, Editorial Work-Scholar; Stevan Baron, Production Director; Linda Tarack, Production Associate.

Project editor: Robert Booth

Book design by Robert W. Madden

Aperture Foundation, Inc., publishes a periodical, books, and portfolios of fine photography to communicate with serious photographers and creative people everywhere. A complete catalog is available upon request. Address: 20 East 23 Street, New York, New York, 10010.

END SHEETS—SCULPTED POLES KNOWN AS *ALO ALO* MARK A MAHAFALY GRAVE NEAR BETIOKY.